THIRTEEN MONTHS
IN
DIXIE,
OR, THE
ADVENTURES OF
A FEDERAL PRISONER
IN
TEXAS

William Francis Oscar Federhen

Jeaninne Surette Honstein and
Steven A. Knowlton, editors

SB

Savas Beatie
California

First edition, first printing

Library of Congress Cataloging-in-Publication Data

Names: Federhen, W. F. Oscar, 1846 – author. | Honstein, Jeaninne Surette, editor. | Knowlton, Steven A. (Steven Anthony), 1971 – editor.
Title: Thirteen months in Dixie: or, Adventures of a Federal Prisoner in Texas, including the Red River Campaign, Imprisonment at Camp Ford, and Escape Overland to Liberated Shreveport, 1864-1865 / by W. F. Oscar Federhen; edited by Jeaninne Surette Honstein and Steven A. Knowlton.
Other titles: Adventures of a Federal Prisoner in Texas
Description: El Dorado Hills, CA: Savas Beatie LLC, [2022] | Includes bibliographical references and index. | Summary: "Oscar Federhen of the 13th Massachusetts Light Artillery was captured by Confederate soldiers during the Red River Campaign in the spring of 1864. Federhen was marched overland to Tyler, Texas, where he was held as a prisoner of war in Camp Ford but later escaped to Union lines. After the war, Federhen wrote a memoir of his wartime experiences. This book contains his transcribed and annotated manuscript with illustrations, including two from Federhen's own pen." — Provided by publisher.
Identifiers: LCCN 2022007400 | ISBN 9781611215885 (hardcover) | ISBN 9781611215892 (ebook)
Subjects: LCSH: United States–History–Civil War, 1861-1865–Personal narratives. | United States–History–Civil War, 1861-1865–Prisoners and prisons. | Camp Ford (Tex.) | Prisoner-of-war escapes–Texas–History–19th century. | Escaped prisoners of war–United States–Biography. | Soldiers–United States–Diaries. | United States. Army. Massachusetts Infantry Regiment, 13th

Savas Beatie
989 Governor Drive, Suite 102,
El Dorado Hills, CA 95762
916-941-6896 / sales@savasbeatie.com / www.savasbeatie.com

Proudly published, printed, and warehoused in the United States of America.

Jeannine Surette Honstein dedicates this book:

To my father, William Federhen Surette, and his "Aunty" Lizzy Federhen.

To my mother, Margaret S. Surette, for the inspiration to do family research.

With love to my husband, Robert.

For our grandchildren Hazel, Henry, Judy and Teddy.

Steven A. Knowlton dedicates this book:

To the memory of those who fought and died for liberty and union—now and forever,
one and inseparable—that remembrance of their devotion to the last best
hope of earth may strengthen our own resolve to
preserve democracy in the present age.

W. F. OSCAR FEDERHEN

Postwar portrait from a composite photograph with portraits of 116
members of the John A. Logan Post No. 127 of the Grand Army of the
Republic in Salina, Kansas, c. 1911.

Smoky Hill Museum Object Identification Number 1946.12.1. Donated by
Cora Walker Shelton to the Smoky Hill Museum, Salina, Kansas.

TABLE of CONTENTS

CONTENTS (CONTINUED)

LIST OF MAPS

LIST OF PHOTOS AND ILLUSTRATIONS

blood, we mounted our horses
and rode on. we changed our
course and started back toward
camp on another road, the we rode
that day and slept in a barn
at night the next day we stopped
at houses and got our meals
and got a good supply of meat
and wheat for the camp
without costing anything instead
of going direct back to camp
we took a road north of where
the camp was so as to see the
place where the yanks were killed
a few days before, we reached
there the next day and it was
just as they had left it. the
body's lay piled on on top of
the other and was a heart sick
sight to look at. the birds and
wild hogs had been feasting
from their bodies and their faces

INTRODUCTION

IT WAS in 2015 when my father told me he had a Civil War manuscript. This memoir was passed to him through his adoptive parent he affectionately called "Aunty." The manuscript belonged to Aunty's father, William Francis Oscar Federhen, a Civil War prisoner who wrote about his remarkable experiences during the conflict.

When Aunty passed in 1951, my father found a tin box with two manuscripts inside. They were a common type of journal that people used in the 1800s. My father took the box home and forgot about it until 2015 when he passed the books to me.

I found the story almost fantastical, and it certainly grabbed my full attention. I dove deep into the pages trying to validate as much as I could. I tried to map his escape routes and follow his descriptions. I often

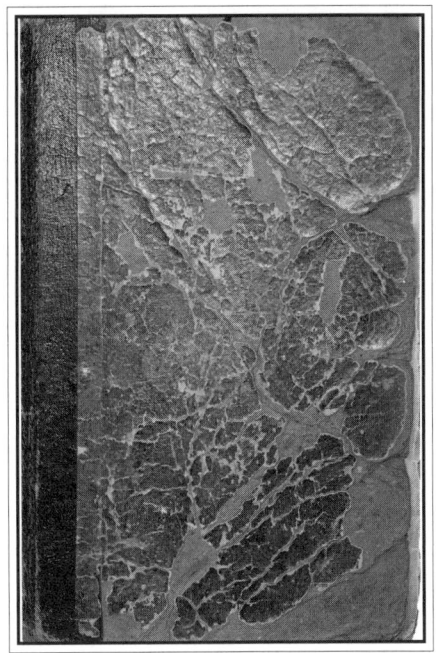

Binding of Federhen's
revised manuscript.

Jeaninne Surette Honstein

described his capture from along the Red River, his life as a prisoner, and his escapes from his captors. The research led me down many new paths and opened my eyes to a part of the Civil War completely new to me.

At one point I asked my father if he remembered Oscar. His only memory—a very distant one—is of an old man in the side room of their apartment. He remembers seeing medicine bottles and something about his feet being of certain concern; the aging veteran lay in a bed with a sheet tented over his feet. My father turned five in January of 1933, the same year Oscar passed away.

With the manuscripts in my possession, I did as much research as I could. I am not a seasoned Civil War researcher and knew I needed help validating much of what Oscar had written. I reached out to Anne Jarvis, Princeton University Librarian, who connected me with Steven A. Knowlton, Librarian for History and African American Studies at the same institution. Steve proved an excellent partner on this project. Once he had the manuscript in hand, he jumped right in and validated more details than I believed possible.

Throughout this project I kept thinking about how connected we are to the past. I find it particularly amazing that, here I am, sitting with my father who personally knew someone who fought in the Civil War. His recollection as a young child of having to be quiet when the old man was sleeping gives me chills, yet at the same time enlightens me to realize the war was really not that long ago, and how necessary it is to remember this.

Jeaninne Surette Honstein

EDITORS' PREFACE

THE TEXT that follows was transcribed from a manuscript prepared by W. F. Oscar Federhen, a Union soldier in the Civil War who served in 1864 and 1865.

Federhen probably wrote his first draft after 1869 because the notebook in which he wrote his recollections was

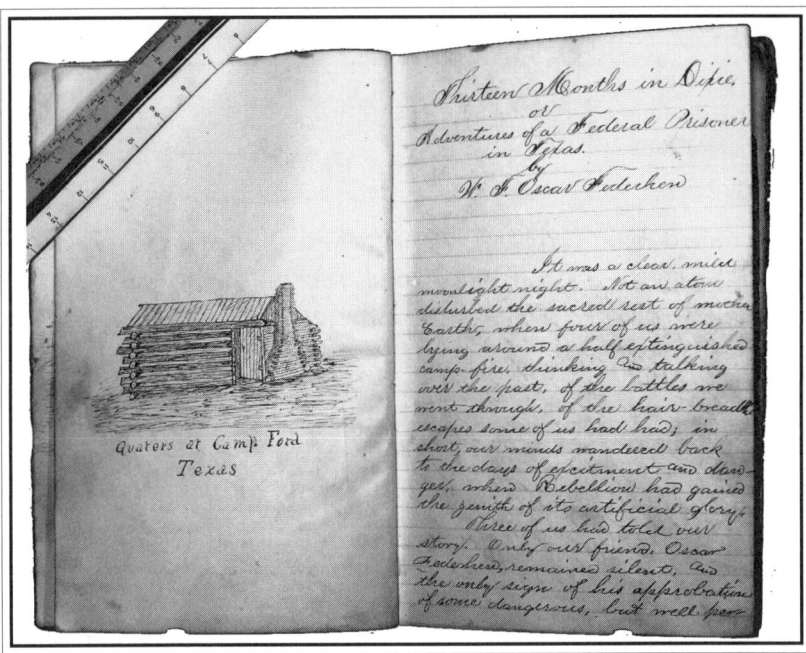

A spread from Federhen's first draft depicting one of his original drawings.

Jeaninne Surette Honstein

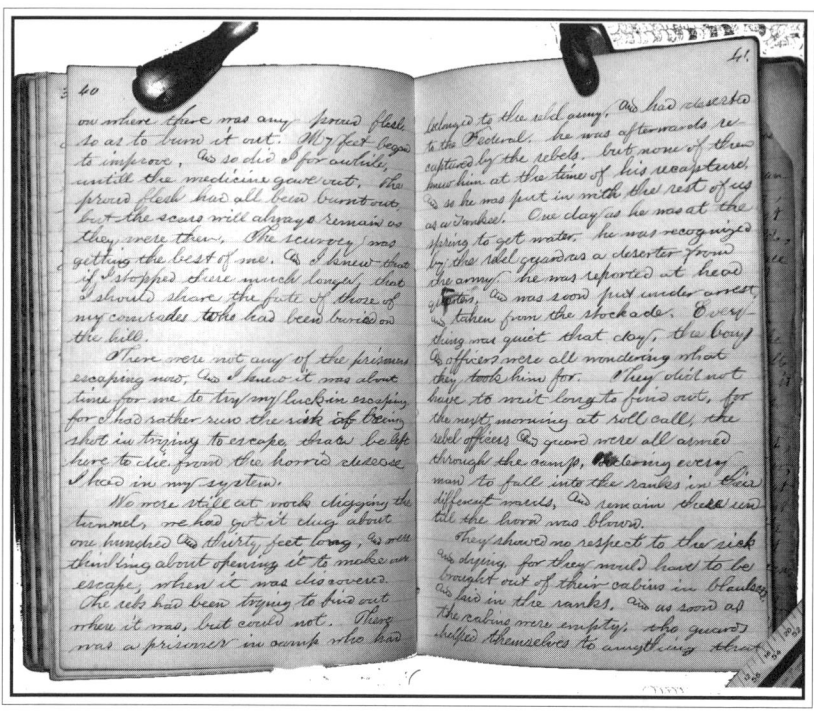

A two-page spread from Federhen's first draft.

Jeaninne Surette Honstein

purchased from George B. Brown and Co., Stationers, of 94 State Street in Boston. According to existing city directories, that business was located at that address between 1869 and 1872.

There is some evidence that the primary composition of the manuscript probably occurred around 1877. In his initial first-draft version of the manuscript, Federhen ends his narrative during his second imprisonment in Bonham, Texas, and then proceeds, as he puts it, to "coppy from a Kansas newspaper the Sack of Lawrence, by the noted Guerilla Quantral, written by Maj. John Edwards of Missouri, an Ex Confederate." As it turns out, an article on that very

A two-page spread from Federhen's revised manuscript.

Jeaninne Surette Honstein

topic was published in the *Saline County Journal* of Salina, Kansas, on March 8, 1877.[1]

At a later unknown date Federhen made a fair copy that also revised his earlier draft. The transcription you are about to read was made from the second version of his text. The revisions consist of rephrasing sentences and paragraphs. There was no important stories added or removed up through

---

1 Federhen may have seen the article "The Sack of Lawrence from Its Inception to Its Ghastly Culmination," published in the *Saline County Journal* (Salina, Kansas) on March 8, 1877. According to the paper, the story was originally filed by the *Chicago Times'* St. Louis correspondent.

the point at which the first draft terminated. The conclusion of the narrative appears only in the second draft.

Both manuscripts were passed down through Federhan's dependents until they were held by Oscar's adopted grandson, William Federhen Surette. William passed them to his daughter, Jeaninne Surette Honstein of Princeton, New Jersey. Jeaninne transcribed the revised manuscript, and Steven A. Knowlton annotated the document in 2017 and 2018. The spelling, punctuation, and grammar of the manuscript have been preserved. Chapter titles were added by the editors.

Convoluted punctuation and grammar notwithstanding, Federhen's narrative is a compelling tale. His keen eye for detail is novelistic in its flair, and his ability to convey desperation and danger in just a few words would have made him a successful writer of dime novels. There is a powerful flow to the story such that a reader cannot help but worry about and cheer for Federhen during his many escapades. His account of the last months of the Civil War carry with it a vividness that most non-fiction accounts rarely aspire to achieve.

While many key elements and observations Federhen recorded can be confirmed by the historical record, others are more suspect. In at least one instance, Federhen claims to have encountered historical figures who could not have been in the place he described at the time he claims to have been there. Notorious Confederate guerrilla leader William T. "Bloody Bill" Anderson, for example, was dead by the time Federhen claims he made his way into Indian Territory, and William Quantrill's Raiders had dispersed into Missouri, Kentucky, and Tennessee by the time Federhen writes about riding with them.

Similar problems arise trying to corroborate Federhen's stories of escape from various Confederate installations, but that is unsurprising given the sparse nature of Southern record keeping during the last year of the war, and especially in that part of the Trans-Mississippi Theater. Some of Federhen's escapes seem fanciful, but they correspond with the accounts of other escapees such Aaron Sutton and S. A. Swiggett.[2]

His stories of robbery, murder, and mayhem were not uncommon in that region, especially during the ending months of the Civil War when irregulars, guerillas, and outright criminals roamed the prairies from Missouri all the way south to the Rio Grande. We know with certainty that he was captured in May of 1864 and returned as a prisoner of war about a year later. He spent those eventful months doing *something, somewhere,* and his version of what he did and where is inside these pages.

Readers will have to judge for themselves the reliability of Federhen's account; we have faith few will deny that it is a gripping tale and one you won't soon forget.

---

2 See, for example, David G. MacLean, ed., *Prisoner of the Rebels in Texas: The Civil War Narrative of Aaron T. Sutton* (Decatur, IN: Americana Books, 1978), and S. A. Swiggett, *The Bright Side of Prison Life* (Baltimore: Fleet, McGinley, & Co., 1897).

BIOGRAPHICAL NOTE ON
W. F. OSCAR FEDERHEN AND FAMILY

WILLIAM FRANCIS Oscar Federhen (rhymes with "veteran") was born in the 1840s in Boston, Massachusetts, to Jacob and Elizabeth Federhen. Jacob worked as a jeweler in Boston for most of his life and died in 1860.

Oscar's exact age is a small mystery. He declared a birth date of September 17, 1844, at his enlistment. His gravestone, however, has 1843 as his year of birth, but he claimed he was 21 when he got married on January 1, 1867. An older brother, William F. Federhen, was born in 1841 and died four years later in 1845 from croup. As a result, it seems likely that William Francis Oscar Federhen was born in 1846 and named for his late brother. Oscar's other siblings included Jacob (born 1839), Anna (1840-1922), George (Jan. 26, 1850), and Frank (1854).[1]

Oscar's brother Jacob enlisted in the 1st Massachusetts Light Artillery on April 20, 1861, for 90 days and was immediately dispatched to Baltimore to preserve the federal government's control over the city. (Jacob's early enlistment

---

1 Ancestry.com: Massachusetts, U.S., Town and Vital Records, 1620-1988.

qualified him for the Massachusetts Minute Man Medal, issued in 1902.) He reenlisted for three years with the rank of Quartermaster Sergeant on August 28, 1861. The history of Jacob's battery is one of continuous engagement. It saw service with the Army of the Potomac in nearly every major battle in the Eastern Theater. He was promoted to 2nd Lt. on September 23, 1861, and 1st Lt. a year later after Crampton's Gap. He was wounded through both thighs at Spotsylvania in May 1864 and mustered out of service that October 19.[2]

Jacob lived in Boston after the war, married, and moved to Kansas. In 1885 he filed for a pension as an invalid and received $12.75 per month. He died on November 28, 1915.

As for Oscar, nothing of substance is known of his prewar years. He appeared on a list of men subject to the draft in May or June of 1863 and enlisted as a private in the 13th Independent Battery, Massachusetts Light Artillery on March 25, 1864, noting his occupation as "brass finisher." U.S. Army records indicate that he was made a prisoner of war on May 3, 1864, "while en route to battery," and that he "escaped on June 3, 1865."

After he rejoined his battery during the waning days of war, Oscar was mustered out on July 28, 1865. The U.S. Army confirmed his status as a prisoner of war.

---

2 Massachusetts Adjutant General's Office, *Massachusetts Soldiers, Sailors, and Marines in the Civil War* (Norwood, MA: Norwood Press), 1931; Dean Sargent, *Grand Army of the Republic: Civil War Veterans, Department of Massachusetts, 1866 to 1947* (Bowie, MD: Heritage Books, 2002); Ancestry.com: Massachusetts, Birth Records, 1840–1915; Massachusetts, Town and Vital Records, 1620–1988; Massachusetts, State Census, 1865; Massachusetts, Mason Membership Cards, 1733–1990; Kansas, Grand Army of the Republic Post Reports, 1880–1940; U.S. City Directories, 1822–1995; U.S., Civil War Pension Index: General Index to Pension Files, 1861–1934; U.S. Civil War Soldiers, 1861–1865; U.S. Civil War Soldier Records and Profiles, 1861– 1865; U.S., Civil War Draft Registrations Records, 1863–1865.

A Capsule History of the 13th Independent Battery, Massachusetts Light Artillery

The 13th Independent Battery served in the Civil War from late 1862 until end of the conflict. It had a complement of 355 men during the duration of the war. Light artillery commands like this battery were mobile and served in the field alongside infantry and cavalry, as opposed to heavy artillery units, which were stationed in fixed fortifications.[1]

The 13th battery was raised by Timothy W. Terry and rendezvoused at Camp Meigs in Boston on October 27, 1862. It was under Capt. Charles H. J. Hamlin when it set out by sea for New Orleans on January 20, 1863. After short stormy voyage, during which many of the battery's horses were killed, the ship put in at Fortress Monroe at the tip of the

---

1 Information about the 13th Massachusetts Light Artillery is compiled from the following sources: James L. Bowen, *Massachusetts in the War, 1861–1865* (Springfield, Mass: Clark W. Bryan & Co., 1889); Massachusetts Adjutant General's Office, *Massachusetts Soldiers, Sailors, and Marines in the Civil War* (Norwood, Mass.: Norwood Press, 1931); *Annual Report of the Adjust-ant-General, of the Commonwealth of Massachusetts, with reports from the Quartermaster-General, Surgeon- General, and Master of Ordnance* (Boston: Wright & Potter), for the years 1863, 1864, and 1865.

Virginia Peninsula. The men and animals spent the next six weeks there recuperating. The artillery outfit finally reached New Orleans on May 10.

During the summer of 1863, the battery turned its horses over to another command and shipped north with the rest of Maj. Gen. Nathaniel Banks' XIX Corps (Department of the Gulf) to besiege the 7,500 Confederate defenders of Port Hudson, a strong bastion on the Mississippi River below Vicksburg. The men of the 13th Independent Battery served four stationary mortars and bombarded the enemy for 31 days straight. The grueling siege lasted 48 days and was the longest in American history. The Southern strongpoint finally surrendered on July 9. Wounds and disease had reduced the 13th to about 50 men, or roughly one-third of its normal strength.

Following a period of rest, the 13th merged briefly with the 2nd Independent Battery, Massachusetts Light Artillery, and took part in Second Bayou Teche expedition in western Louisiana in September and October of 1863 before wintering in New Iberia and Franklin. In March of 1864, the artillerists of the 13th Independent Battery were attached to Battery L, 1st U.S. Artillery, and participated in the General Banks' disastrous Red River Campaign. The objective was to move up the Red River, capture Shreveport, and destroy Confederate forces operating in the region and confiscate Southern cotton. The low water in the Red River stranded the Union fleet and Banks was routed at Mansfield on April 8, though he managed to blunt Confederate attacks the next day at Pleasant Hill. Banks had little choice but to retreat to Alexandria to save his command. The 13th Battery saw combat during the campaign at Pleasant Hill on April 9, at the Cane River Crossing on April 19, and again at Marksville Plains on May 13.

It was during this period of the war that W. F. Oscar Federhen was recruited to the battery as a replacement. He was on his way to join the 13th, which was camped at

Alexandria, when he was taken prisoner on May 3. Federhen never saw combat with the 13th Independent Battery. The artillery unit returned to New Orleans on June 29 and remained there for the duration of the war. After escaping from a Confederate prison camp in Texas, Federhen rejoined the unit during its final days of service. Once the war ended, Oscar and the rest of the battery returned to Massachusetts and were mustered out on July 28, 1865. During the war, the 13th battery lost one man killed in action and 27 to disease.[2]

2 For additional detailed information on the 13th Independent Battery than the sources earlier cited, see Frederick H. Dyer, *A Compendium of the War of the Rebellion* (Morningside: Dayton, OH: 1978), 25, 157, 550, 551, 553, 556, 1247.

THIRTEEN MONTHS IN DIXIE,
OR, THE ADVENTURES OF A
FEDERAL PRISONER IN TEXAS

by W. F. Oscar Federhen

IT WAS a clear, mild moonlight night. Not an atom disturbed the sacred rest of mother Earth, when four of us were lying around a half extinguished camp-fire, thinking and talking over the past, of the battles we went through, of the hair-breadth escapes some of us had had; in short, our minds wandered back to the days of excitement and danger, when Rebellion had gained the zenith of its artificial glory.

Three of us had told our story. Only our friend, Oscar Federhen, remained silent, and the only sign of his approbation of some dangerous, but well performed duty, was a slight nod of the head, and a double cloud of smoke, emerging from out of his wooden pipe, the soldier's only reliable friend and companion. After much persuading and coaxing, we gained his consent to narrate his history to us. This gained, we replenished our pipes, and, after having lighted them, Oscar began.[1]

---

1 This Introduction purports to be composed by another narrator, but it is written in the same hand (i.e., Oscar's) as the rest of the manuscript.

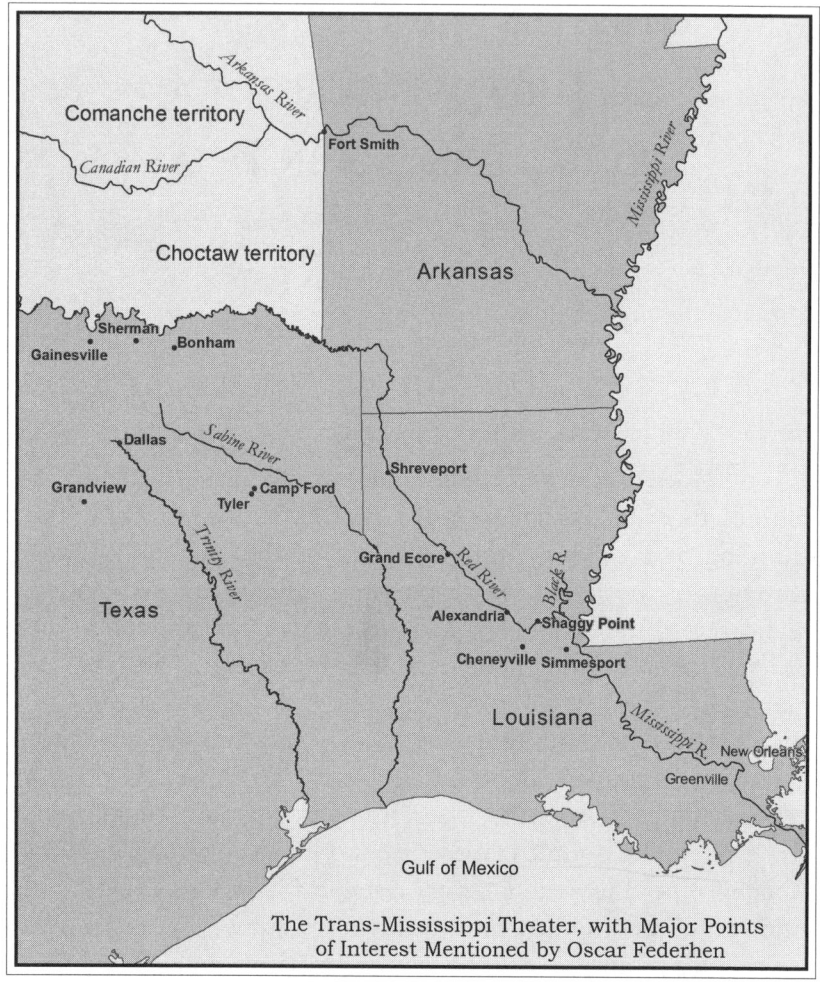

Wangyal Shawa

Comanche territory

Arkansas River

Canadian River

Fort Smith

Choctaw territory

Arkansas

Mississippi River

Sherman
Bonham
Gainesville

Dallas

Sabine River

Shreveport

Grandview

Camp Ford
Tyler

Trinity River

Grand Ecore

Red River

Black R.

Texas

Alexandria
Shaggy Point

Cheneyville
Simmesport

Louisiana

Mississippi R.

New Orleans

Greenville

Gulf of Mexico

The Trans-Mississippi Theater, with Major Points
of Interest Mentioned by Oscar Federhen

1

ENLISTMENT AND
TRANSPORT TO LOUISIANA
(MARCH AND APRIL 1864)

WHEN THIS perfidious rebellion began, I was engaged in some affair, the negligence of which would have utterly ruined me, but as soon as I could safely do so, I offered my services at the altar of Liberty for my beloved country. I enlisted March 25th, 1864 in and for the City of Boston, Mass., the place where I was born, reared and educated, and was sent to Galloup's island[1] on the same day, to await the departure of a steamer for New Orleans, as the 13th Mass, battery, Lieut. Nichols commanding, in which I had enlisted, had been stationed in Louisiana, ever since the siege of Port Hudson.[2]

---

1 Gallop's Island is located in Boston Harbor. During the Civil War, the city of Boston loaned Gallop's Island to the federal government, which used it as a rendezvous point for newly enlisted soldiers. Nathaniel B. Shurtleff, *A Topographical and Historical Description of Boston*, 2nd ed. (Boston: Noyes, Holmes, and Co., 1872), 547.

2 See "A Capsule History of the 13th Independent Battery Massachusetts Light Artillery" that begins on page xviii for more information on this organization. In 1864, Robert C. Nichols of Boston served as second lieutenant with the Thirteenth Battery, Light Artillery.

On the 6th of April, 1864, I took passage for the "sunny south," and arrived at New Orleans on the 21st inst.,[3] here I rested until the 25th, when I started on board the "Rob Roy" up the Mississippi for Alexandria, La., then the rendezvous of my battery.[4]

In the afternoon of the 28th we arrived at the mouth of the Black River, on Red River, and remained there until a boat should come down from Alexandria, and report the banks free from Guerillas.[5] I had not been on land for some time, and longed very much to have solid earth once more under my feet.

On the 30th, the boat was moored about six yards from the shore, and when a board was laid out for one of the officers to go on shore, and five others and myself, improved the opportunity, and went also. The captain cautioned us not to go too far, because he expected to start every hour. We rambled about the country for about an hour and a half, when the boat blew the signal to board. We started on a run, but came too late, the steamer had gone, and left us behind.

We made signals to the gunboat stationed nearby, and the commander of her took us on board to await the coming of

---

3 "Inst." is an abbreviation for the Latin phrase *instante mense*, meaning "this month" (that is, April). George Roberts, *The Terms and Language of Trade and Commerce, and of the Business of Every-Day Life* (London: Longman, Orme, Brown, Green, and Longmans, 1841), 25.

4 The *Rob Roy* was a wooden transport steamboat. It was a privately owned vessel, pressed into service by the U.S. Army from Mar. 19, 1864, through some time in the summer of 1864. It carried four Parrott guns (rifled artillery pieces; the size of the guns on the *Rob Roy* is unspecified). Gary D. Joiner, *Through the Howling Wilderness: The 1864 Red River Campaign and Union Failure in the West* (Knoxville: University of Tennessee Press, 2006), 189; Charles Dana Gibson and E. Kay Gibson, *Dictionary of Transports and Combatant Vessels, Steam and Sail, Employed by the Union Army, 1861–1868* (Camden, ME: Ensign Press, 1995), 273.

5 About one mile south of present-day Acme, LA.

The 1st New York Light Artillery (also known as Morgan's Light Artillery),
a prototypical battery of Union guns.

Library of Congress

the next transport to send us up the river.[6] We did marine's
duty during our stay on board.[7]

6 This may have been the U.S.S. *Avenger* or the U.S.S. *Vindicator*, both of
which were anchored at the mouth of the Black River at various times in
late Apr. and early May of 1864. *Official Records of the Union and
Confederate Navies in the War of the Rebellion*, 30 vols. (Washington, DC:
Government Printing Office, 1894), Series I, vol. 26, pp. 103, 239. Hereafter
cited as *OR Navies*. All references are to Series I unless otherwise stated.

7 In the nineteenth century, explained one historian, marines "served on
board . . . as ship's police, and, when engaged in battle, boarded the enemy
or prevented him from doing the same." David M. Sullivan, *The United
States Marine Corps in the Civil War*, 2 vols. (Shippensburg, PA: White Mane
Publishing Co., 1997), vol. 1: *The First Year*, xi.

A large river steamer turned into a troop transport ship
arriving in New Orleans during the Civil War.

Harper's Weekly, January 10, 1863

The *City Belle* (left) next to the *Calypso*.

Image Courtesy of Keith Norrington

On the evening of May 2, the steamer "City Bell" came past and was signaled from the gun-boat to lay to, she complied with the order, and, after having taken us on board, steamed up the river as self-reliant and independent as could be.[8]

---

8 The *City Belle* was a wooden stern wheel pressed into duty by the U.S. Army from May 1–15, 1864. It was shorter than 200 feet, had a capacity of 600, and was unarmed. In the first week of May 1864, the *City Belle* was assigned to transport the 120th Ohio to Alexandria. The ship also "picked up a hundred more troops belonging to other units" who may have included members of the 73rd U.S. Colored Troops. Joiner, *Through the Howling Wilderness*, 189; Gibson and Gibson, *Dictionary of Transports and Combatant Vessels*, 60; *OR Navies* XXVI/1/117; *OR Navies* 24/3/115; Jean Powers Soman and Frank L. Byrne, eds., *A Jewish Colonel in the Civil War. Marcus M. Spiegel of the Ohio Volunteers* (University of Nebraska Press, 1995), 335; Frederick Phisterer, *StatisticalRecord of the Armies of the United States. Campaigns of the Civil War* (New York: Charles Scribner's Sons, 1883), 172.

Confederate troops attacking a Union gunboat
during the 1864 Red River Campaign.

Harper's Weekly, May 14, 1864

2

CAPTURED BY CONFEDERATE TROOPS

(MAY 3, 1864)

ON MAY the 3rd about half past four in the afternoon, we made "Snaky Point,"[1] and found the banks occupied by Confederate Gen. Lane's division and some artillery.[2]

As soon as we hove in sight, we received the fire of their artillery, and one of the first shots went through our boilers,

1 Snaggy Point, also known as Davide's Ferry, is on the Red River in Louisiana thirty miles below Alexandria near present-day Moncla.

2 These may have been the First Texas Partisan Rangers, a cavalry unit under the command of Col. Walter Paye Lane. Lane would not have been present because he was injured during the Battle of Mansfield on Apr. 8. Lane's second in command was Lt. Col. Richard P. Crump. Lane's regiment, part of Brig. Gen. James P. Major's brigade, was posted to Davide's Ferry on Apr. 30 and destroyed several Union boats over the following week. Federhen may be referring to the entire brigade, which during the latter phase of the Red River Campaign was nominally under the command of Lane, who as major assumed temporary command of a division of cavalry. Jimmy L. Bryan, *More Zeal Than Discretion: The Westward Adventures of Walter P. Lane* (College Station: Texas A&M University Press, 2008), 137–40; Joiner, *Through the Howling Wilderness*, 194; Richard Taylor, *Destruction and Reconstruction: Personal Experiences of the Late War* (New York: D. Appleton and Co., 1879), 185; Ralph A. Wooster, *Lone Star Regiments in Gray* (Austin, TX: Eakin Press, 2002), 181–82.

disabling the boat immediately.[3] We had only infantry on board, and many of those got burned or otherwise injured by the escaping steam, so our resistance was but feeble, and, after an half-hours' fighting, the Johnnies came on board.[4]

I was standing near the cabin, and trying to get as much as possible into my haversack, for I knew a hard fate was before me. I had just packed away a splendid revolver, when a confederate stepped up to me and said, "Say, you hound, do you have a revolver?"

"No," said I.

"Well, let me see what you have there in your haversack." And, adding action to words, he took it from me and after fumbling a little, he brought out my revolver. He got infuriated, and said he was going to shoot me, when I, feeling myself outraged, cried out to him, "Shoot away then, you thieving scoundrel," and I am convinced that the courage I showed him saved my life, for he came down somewhat and said, "Let me see them boots o' yours, I guess they would fit me very well." What could I do, unarmed as I was, but obey. He put my new boots on his feet, but instead of giving me his old pair of shoes, the "gentleman of the south" threw them overboard.

3 Naval officers reported on May 4 that "the transport *City Belle* was captured and destroyed by the rebels about 30 miles above Fort De Russy. She had on board an Ohio regiment . . . all of whom, with the exception of half a dozen, were captured or killed. They made a gallant fight, I am informed." An Army officer told colleagues that the *City Belle* was "destroyed by batteries about 20 miles above Fort De Russy. One hundred and twentieth Ohio on board. The loss of this regiment I understand to be one-third." Other reports estimated that of the 700 men in the 120th, 150 escaped capture. The federal government later paid $15,000 to the owner of *City Belle* for the loss of his vessel. *OR Navies*, I/XXVI:107, 108, 123; Gibson and Gibson, *Dictionary of Transports and Combatant Vessels*, 60.

4 Johnny (short for Johnny Reb) was a nickname for a Confederate soldier. Wright, *The Language of the Civil War*, 164.

"Hollo, a nice jacket you have got on, Yank; I reckon it would suit me a darned sight better than you." So off comes my jacket. Through this, he saw my gold watch chain, and with a yell of Satanic pleasure he said, "What? You sport a watch? Will you let me see what it is made of? Gold? That will shine a great deal better on Confederate grey, than on your cussed blue. Got anything else? Some money?" After having taken my watch and chain, he thrust his dirty fingers into my pockets, and took all the money I had, besides knife, comb, etc., etc. Just at this moment the order was given to bring us prisoners on shore.

The confederate soldiers then drove us like so many sheep with the point of the bayonet or the butt of the musket into the deep river. Whoever could swim, came on shore, but only to fall from Scylla into Charybitis.[5] How many got drowned, I cannot guess.

What made me surrender all my personal property so quietly was that I had seen men shot down on the boat for refusing to deliver their property. Happily I reached the shore, where, with the rest who had been saved, I had to pass through a double line of "Johnnies." I was then barefooted and had nothing left on me but shirt, pants, and a new hat, which I had bought in New Orleans. I was quite at the end of the line. A Reb took hold of my hat, with the words: "Give me that hat, you cussed Yankee hound." There I was now, nothing on me but a shirt and a pair of pants. An old Rebel took pity on me and said. "Here is an old straw hat that will shade you a little." I turned to thank him, but he was gone. And now begins the life of misery I was destined to lead for thirteen months; months of misery, hunger and sickness. Roasted in the Southern sun by day, chilled to the very

---

5 Between Scylla and Charybdis is an idiom deriving from Greek mythology, meaning, "between two equal dangers." E. Cobham Brewer, *Dictionary of Phrase and Fable* (New York: Cassell and Company, 1898), 9.

marrows by the heavy dews at night. Often for days without food, even water, without shelter, friendless, deserted, lonesome, alone! – months of danger and peril, outrage and hardship.

3

MARCHED TO CAMP FORD

(MAY 5–22, 1864)

WE MARCHED during the entire night, next day, and next night again, and another dreary day until evening without rest, without food. I was barefooted, and never having learned the art of walking in one's natural shoes, you can imagine how sore, and blistered my feet got, and yet it was sure death to lie down. I have seen men on this forced march give out from hunger and fatigue. They begged for only five minutes rest, and received curses and blows in answer. If they could not go further and sank down in the road, the next passing rebel raised his musket, and with the butt smashed out the brains of the unfortunate sufferer. This is no exaggeration, nor did it happen once or twice, but every one unable to track his miserable limbs further, was doomed to the same fate. They would not even waste a bullet on the prostrate man to let him die the death of a soldier and a man. No! They were slaughtered, as you would a mad dog or a poisonous snake.

At last we arrived at Jeneville, in the evening of May 5th.[1] Here we had the first rest granted and also the first rations issued. Rations you would not give to your cur. They gave us

---

1 Cheneyville is on Bayou Boeuf, about nineteen miles south of Snaggy Point.

coarse corn meal, stumps and all ground together, and about two ounces of raw bacon, filthy and actually stinking. May the 6th we started early again on our dreary and for many of us fatal march. But from date to our arrival at Grand Ecore, La., they gave us at least every night one pint of said corn and two ounces of bacon; furthermore, we had five to six hours rest every night.[2] We had to mix our meal with water, and lay the paste on a stone or board before the fire to bake it. Salt was, of course, an unknown luxury. The meat we had to lay in the fire to kill the darling little creatures who in their innocence had made our rations their head-quarters.

At Grand Ecore we were driven on board the boat and the banner of treason flying above us. We started up the Red River for Shreveport, where we arrived May 16, half famished.[3] But there was no rest, no food, no kindly word to help us along; on the contrary, we had to march towards Taylor, Texas, as soon as we had been landed.

On we staggered day and night, with hardly any rest for five days. Woe to the man whose power of endurance left him. His fate was sealed. So we travelled 115 miles in five days, sore and sick, and half crazy with hunger as we were.[4] Then the walls of the stockade took us into its cold, chilly arms, out of which nine tenths came only as corpses.[5] There was then

---

2 Grand Ecore (French for "great bluff") is on the Red River about 80 miles northwest of Cheneyville. The prisoners were required to march rather than travel by water because Union forces were still in control of the Red River up to Alexandria.

3 Shreveport is about seventy miles upstream from Grand Ecore.

4 Using modern highways (Interstate 20), Shreveport is ninety-eight miles from Tyler. It may have been longer to travel by foot in 1864.

5 In reality, of the approximately 6,000 prisoners confined in Camp Ford at one time or another, 286 died within its walls. This death rate of five percent was low compared to other Confederate prisons. F. Lee Lawrence and Robert W. Glover, *Camp Ford, C.S.A.: The Story of Union Prisoners in*

at Camp Ford, the name of the stockade, over 4000 prisoners huddled together.[6]

Texas (Austin: Texas Civil War Centennial Advisory Committee, 1964), 72–73.

6 Camp Ford was a stockade prison. It current address is 6500 U.S. Route 271 (about four miles northeast of downtown Tyler, Texas). The camp was established in 1862 as a compound for training conscripts for service in the Confederate Army. It began housing prisoners of war on July 30, 1863. Lawrence and Glover, *Camp Ford*, 3–4. "From April until July 9, 1864 . . . the living conditions [at Camp Ford] were shocking. . . . No shelters of any kind were supplied . . . the prisoners were told that they would have to construct their own shelters out of whatever materials were available." In June 1864, 4,527 prisoners were recorded as being present in Camp Ford. Lawrence and Glover, *Camp Ford*, 9–10, 23.

4

HELD PRISONER IN CAMP FORD

(CA. MAY–OCTOBER 1864)

HUNGER AND necessity makes mankind industrious, so I picked up old bones, and, with the assistance of a broken knife, carved out rings, which I sold to my fellow prisoners and to our guard, and through this means I kept myself in a little tobacco, the only consolation or friend, you may say, that the poor prisoner had. The U.S. Sanitary Commission sent through the lines boxes of clothing for us, and we actually received some of it.[1] I received a blouse, a shirt, a pair of shoes and a blanket.

Toward the beginning of August, for now I am unable to give you the day and date any longer, as a diary or calendar is an article utterly unknown in prison, I tried my best to get

---

1 The United States Sanitary Commission consisted of volunteers commissioned by the Secretary of War to provide inspection and assistance to the Union army's efforts to maintain the health, comfort, and cleanliness of the troops. On occasion, the commission was able to work with officials in the Confederate government to pass supplies (such as clothing) through the lines and to soldiers in Confederate prison camps. Camp Ford, for example, received a shipment of 1,200 pairs of shoes, shirts, underwear, and pants on Oct. 5, 1864. William Quentin Maxwell, *Lincoln's Fifth Wheel: The Political History of the United States Sanitary Commission* (New York: Longmans, Green, 1956); Lawrence and Glover, *Camp Ford*, 24.

Union prisoners from Camp Ford. *Library of Congress*

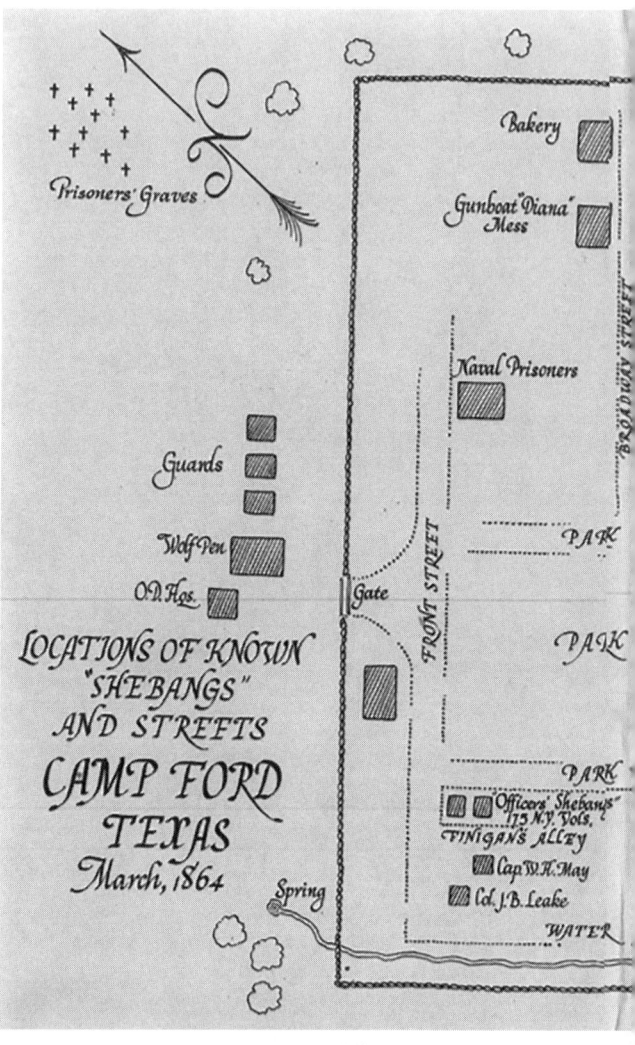

Lawrence and Glover, Camp Ford, C.S.A.

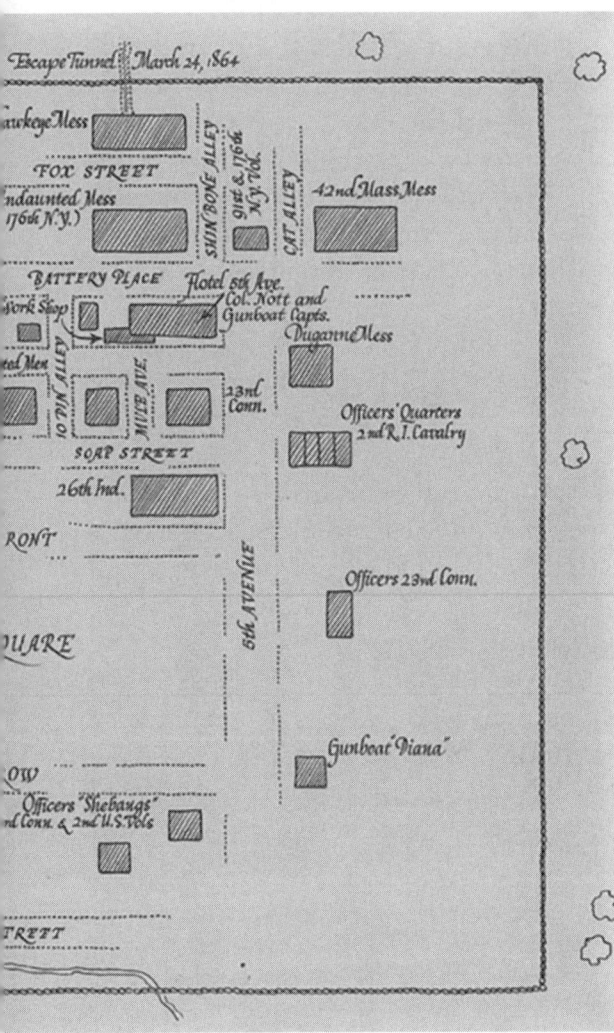

Escape Tunnel March 24, 1864

Hawkeye Mess

FOX STREET

Undaunted Mess
176th N.Y.)

SHIN BONE ALLEY

91st & 176th
N.Y. Vol.

CAT ALLEY

42nd Mass. Mess

BATTERY PLACE   Hotel 5th Ave.
Work Shop   Col. Nott and
                  Gunboat Capts.
                         Duganne Mess

tal Men

10 PIN ALLEY

MULE AVE.

23rd
Conn.

Officers' Quarters
2nd R.I. Cavalry

SOAP STREET

26th Ind.

RONT

6th AVENUE

Officers 23rd Conn.

UARE

OW

Gunboat "Diana"

Officers "Shebangs"
nd Conn. & 2nd U.S. Vols

TREET

acquainted with some of our guards, in which undertaking I succeeded to the detriment of my brass buttons, which article brought his friendship.[2] Toward the middle of August, I had so far won his confidence as to make him an offer of my blanket and blouse, if he would let me escape. He very heartily agreed to it, and one dark night I crept on hands and knees towards the southeast corner of the stockade, where he was stationed as sentinel.

As soon as I arrived there, I called him by name. He demanded the articles of our treaty first, so I threw them over to him, and then crept over myself. We shook hands, and I started on a run for dear life. I knew every moment was precious, and kept on running until morning.

At about eight o'clock, my physical strength left me lying in a swamp underneath a tree. I had been resting about half an hour, when I heard to my horror, the distinct howl of the bloodhounds coming rapidly nearer. Despair gave me strength, and I got up the tree, just in time to be saved from a horrible death. Seven hounds were watching and barking below me, their eyes glittering with the thirst of blood.[3] In a short time two mounted ruffians appeared and wanted to know what business I had up that tree; I answered, "to get out

2 If he were still wearing a regulation uniform, Federhen would have had a uniform jacket with twelve buttons on the placket and a small button on the collar. He may also have had a frock coat with nine buttons on the placket, two small button on the cuffs, and two buttons on the pocket, and an overcoat with around eight buttons (although many soldiers threw these coats away in warm weather), plus a brass cap insignia indicating his role as an artilleryman, and possibly brass "shoulder scales" intended to deflect a saber slash. The buttons would have been stamped with the coat of arms of the state of Massachusetts. It is impossible to know what he was wearing if he had on replacement clothing. Francis A. Lord, *Uniforms of the Civil War* (South Brunswick, NJ: Thomas Yoseloff, 1970), 18–48.

3 Rather than being bloodhounds, the dogs were "of the common East Texas hound variety, used . . . to hunt raccoons and foxes." Lawrence and Glover, *Camp Ford*, 55.

of the way of your infernal dogs." "Come down" halloed one of
them who seemed to be a leader, while the other took a very
unwelcome aim at me with his rifle.

"Call your dogs off then or they will tear me to pieces," I
said. In compliance to my wish, after having muttered some,
to me, not very flattering curses, he recalled them. I more fell,
than crept down, the other ruffian keeping his gun steady
levelled at me, just as if I was a dangerous fellow. They took
me between them and myself, but to no purpose.

As soon as we reached the stockade, I was called before
the commander Col. Boarders. After much damning,
swearing and cursing, he allowed me to return to the

Federhen's sketch of the stockade and mud houses at Camp Ford.

Federhen, first manuscript draft

A woodcut depiction of prisoners and accommodations at Camp Ford.

Harper's Weekly, March 4, 1865

stockade without further punishment. And there I was again, foiled in the dearest hope of my life, and closely watched. But I never thought of giving up the idea that I would escape from them even if it should cost me my life.[4]

I sincerely believe that only this fixed determination kept me alive amongst all the horrors of that prison pen. It rained incessantly for thirteen days and nights. We had no shelter over head, and were almost destitute of clothing. At night, when we laid down to rest, the cold camp ground was our bed, and a log of wood for our pillow, to prevent our head from sinking into the soft ground.

4 Lt. Col. John Pelham Border, who was born in England, served as a captain of the Texas State Troops and later with Texas cavalry. He served as commandant of Camp Ford from May 15 to Aug. 21, 1864. Several postwar accounts depict him as as a harsh officer. Lawrence and Glover, *Camp Ford*, 87; Bruce S. Allardice, *Confederate Colonels: A Biographical Register* (Columbia: University of Missouri Press, 2008), 66.

We lived this way until a new commander was appointed.[5] He allowed us to go into the woods to cut logs to build ourselves cabins; we went in squads of six, having confederate soldiers to guard us. I had got a cabin built. It was eight feet high, and six by ten in width. I lived quite comfortable, for I let a part of my house to three New York soldiers. They were to cook my food and chop wood to pay the rent.

The nights were very cold, I had a fireplace in one side of the house, in which we had to keep a fire all night, to keep us warm, for we had no covering. The earth was banked upon one side of the cabin, and answered for beds. We cooked, ate and slept in this room. Altogether we enjoyed ourselves very well, singing, playing cards and dominoes. "Necessity is the mother of invention." The cards we had were made out of thin pieces of wood with their names and numbers burnt on them by means of a broken fork.

I had everything that was convenient for house- keeping. The dishes, head tray,[6] wash dish, forks and spoons were made out of wood. We lived very well, some days we had a half pint of whole yellow corn, some would boil it or bake it, others would grind or break it between two stones and mix it with a little water and bake it. Some days we would get a little meat or bones, more often the bones, for they gave us the poorest of diseased meat. At night we did not dare to go far from our cabin, for the prisoners were very often shot at by the rebels who were guarding us.

Most of the prisoners, who made their escape, were unfortunate enough to get recaptured either by scouts or

---

5 Col. George Henry Sweet took command of Camp Ford on Aug. 21, 1864. He rose from the rank of private in 1861 to command a cavalry brigade before serving at Camp Ford. Allardice, *Confederate Colonels*, 362.

6 The meaning of "head tray" is unclear and is not found in dictionaries of the period.

A variety of scenes from Camp Ford.

Lawrence and Glover, Camp Ford, C.S.A.

hounds. These were brought back before the rebel commander to await his sentence. Some were strung up by the thumbs (that is, a small cord tied around the thumbs and hoisted over his head, over the limb of a tree, until he could just touch his toes to the ground).[7] I have seen men after they have been let down from this harsh punishment, fall to the ground and would not recover for several days. Others, they would make stand on the stump of a small tree all days without anything to eat.

7 Prisoners from Camp Ford testified about this punishment before a U.S. House of Representatives committee investigating such matters. House of Representatives Report No. 45, *Report on the Treatment of Prisoners of War, by the Rebel Authorities, during the War of the Rebellion* (Washington, DC: Government Printing Office, 1869), 193.

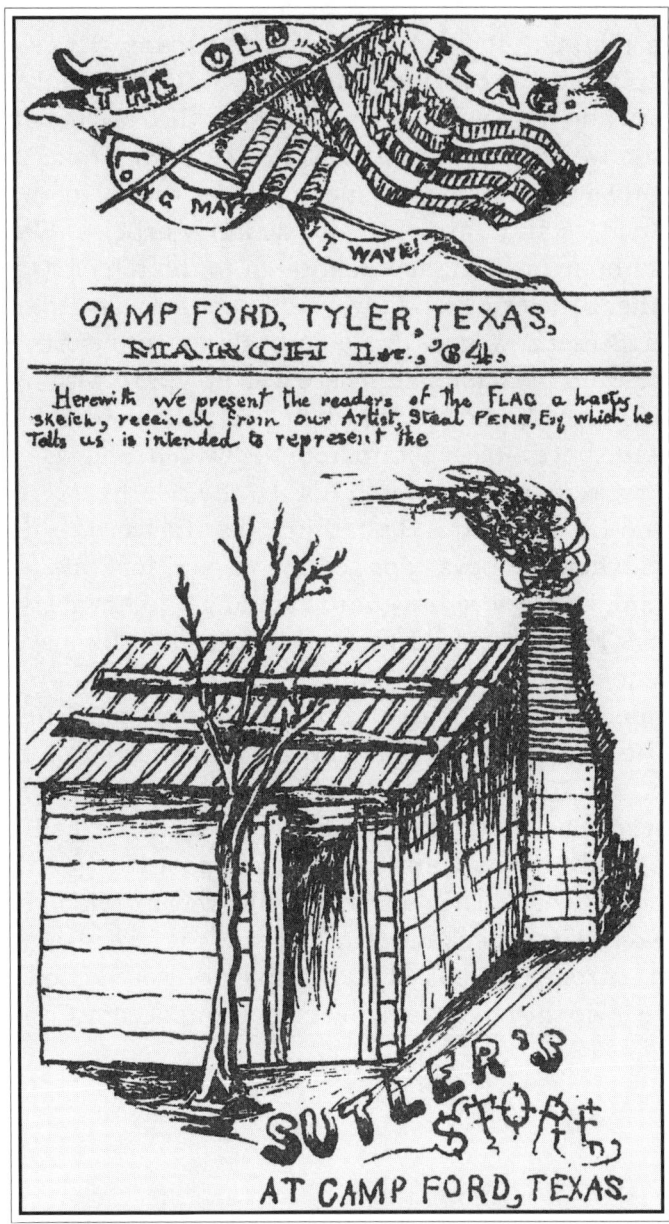

The sutler's store at Camp Ford, as depicted in the camp newspaper *The Old Flag* (March 1, 1864).

Lawrence and Glover, Camp Ford, C.S.A.

We planned all sorts of means to escape. There was a sutler's wagon drove into the camp one day, with sweet potatoes and corn, we had no money, for the rebs took it from us when we were captured, but they could not take Yankee ingenuity away from us. We made powder horns, tooth picks, cigar holders and a number of little fancy articles. We made them of bone or horn, and sold them to the rebs for tobacco and other articles which they would offer for sale. At another time a Sutler's wagon drove into camp with corn, sweet potatoes and meal for sale. There was no guard with him. He was well armed, and thought he could take care of himself. One of the boys stole a potato from the wagon, and was told to put it back, he said he would not, so the reb drew a revolver and said he would fire. He had just got the words out of his mouth, when the boys capsized his wagon, took his revolver from him, and before the guards could get to his assistance; the boys had carried off most of his goods. This gave us a square meal.

Again, a sutler's wagon drove in, and stopped near the gate. He had meal to sell. The boys crowded around his wagon, so as to give to the opportunity of secreting themselves between the coupling pole and the bed of the wagon, and in that manner they rode past the guards and were not detected. They also had a dirt wagon, which carried off the dirt of the stockade. The cart was the size of one of our city dirt carts.[8] The rebs could not spare one of their own men to drive it, so they took an honest fellow out of camp, and gave

---

8 A dirt cart was used to carry away refuse, such as street sweepings, and during this period in the nineteenth century would have included horse droppings. John Russell Bartlett, *Dictionary of Americanisms*, 4th ed. (Boston: Little, Brown, and Co., 1877), 178.

him a parole to drive the cart; the dirt was to be emptied about half a mile from Camp.[9]

The boys would pile a lot of dirt in front of their cabins for the cart to take away. This honest fellow, who drove the cart, got quite rich by carting men, for the boys would give him rings, knives, etc. Two men would like down in the bottom of the cart, and cover their heads with a blanket, then the dirt would be piled on top of them, until there was a load. This Yankee trick was played long enough for about twenty boys to make their escape, when it became known at head-quarters. The morning that it became known, the officer of the guard was stationed at the gate, with orders to thrust his sabre into the dirt, which he did, to the surprise of the inmates. One of them had a sabre thrust through his arm. The rebs were now very angry. They threatened the boys, that, whoever should attempt to escape, or went within ten feet of the stockade, would be shot. After this, they posted a notice in camp, that any Yankee attempting to make his escape from the stockade should be killed, either by the blood-hounds, or by the rebel who caught him. There was no more escaping for some time.[10]

We had a tunnel in operation, which we had been to work on for about four months. There were twenty of us, who were concerned in digging this tunnel. One squad of five would dig half the night and five more the other half; the next night the remaining ten would work the same way. One would dig, and as he dug, he would throw the dirt back of him. Back of him,

---

9 A prisoner who promised not to fight against his captors was released on parole. This usually occurred when the captors lacked the capacity to imprison large numbers of troops. Wright, *The Language of the Civil War*, 223.

10 Other witnesses claim the Confederate authorities discovered this means of jailbreak when one long-legged escapee accidentally exposed a knee above the pile of refuse. Swiggett, *The Bright Side of Prison Life*, 50.

was another man with a haversack which he would fill with the dirt. Another man was at the mouth of the tunnel to receive the haversack as soon as it was filled with dirt. The rope we had was a blanket, cut into strips and tied together. The other two men would carry it off and empty it in holes, or bank it up against their houses. It was very tedious work, for some would not gain more than an inch. The earth was full of large rocks of sandstone, and red clay. We had nothing to dig with but an old common case-knife, and a piece of a sabre.[11] Whenever we had a heavy rain, the water would soak through, into the tunnel, and make it very muddy, so before we could work at digging again, we had to clean this mud all out.

There were four of us who dug, for it required some skill to keep the tunnel level. There were other tunnels in operation, but for want of judgment, they were generally run out of ground before they had got twenty feet from the place they started from. They were always started from a cabin near the stockade. The rebs always found them out, for the boys were not particular enough. They would come out of their cabin in the morning after they had been at work with their clothes all covered with the red clay, and as soon as a Johnny Reb saw them, he well knew what they had been about, and by that means they would get caught. They also knew that there was another tunnel in camp, but could not find it.

They would watch us by day and night. They made an offer to one of the boys if he would tell where the tunnel was. They would give him his parole and send him back to the

---

11 A case knife was a large kitchen or table knife. This method of escape was recorded by Robert Burke of the 67th Indiana Volunteers, whose memoir was privately published in the 1940s. Lyman Cobb, *The Reticule and Pocket Companion, Or, Miniature Lexicon of the English Language* (New York: Harper & Brothers, 1867), 166; Robert Burke, *Escape from a Southern Prison* (n.p., n.d.).

Federal lines. They took one of the boys who had clay on his pants outside the stockade, to get him to tell where the tunnel was, but they found they had got hold of the wrong chap, for he was a true Yankee soldier. He would not tell, so they tied him up by the thumbs, until he turned black in the face, then they let him down to see if he would tell, but he would not, so they tied him up again. When they let him down the second time, he fell to the ground speechless. After he recovered, they asked him again, but he would not tell. He told them he would suffer death in any form, rather than prevent any prisoner from escaping from that miserable pen. After they had nearly killed him and finding they could get nothing out of him, they turned him into the stockades again. Some of the boys felt rather indignant at this, so they called the adjutant hard names as he was going out of the gate.[12] He turned to the prisoners and demanded the man who called him names. He threatened to have all who were standing near the gate shot, if they did not tell who it was, but there was no one who would tell him, so he soon went off to head-quarters, and we did not see anything more of him until afternoon.

The wagon that brought the corn and meal always drove into camp and divided the rations to each man, but on this afternoon the adjutant would not allow it to be driven in. He took the mule out and let the wagon stand outside the stockade, so that we could all see it. He then came into camp with a revolver in his hand, and said he would not let us have anything to eat, until we would tell him who called him

12 An adjutant was an officer with the following duties: "Establishing camps; visiting guards and outposts; mustering and inspecting troops; inspecting guards and detachments; forming parades and line of battle; the conduct and control of deserters and prisoners; making reconnaissances; and in general, discharging such other active duties as may be assigned them." William P. Craighill, *The Army Officer's Pocket Companion: Principally Designed for Staff Officers in the Field* (New York: D. Van Nostrand, 1862), 50–51.

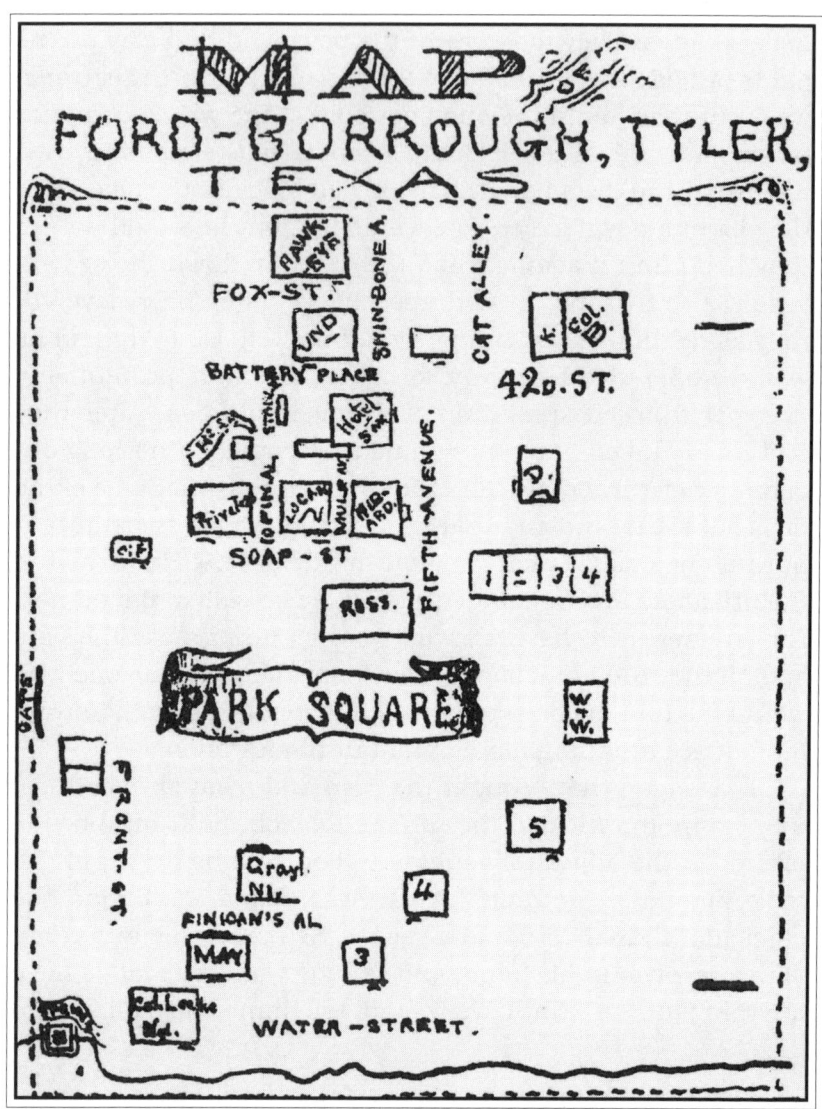

Camp Ford, as depicted in the
camp newspaper *The Old Flag* (March 1, 1864).

Lawrence and Glover, Camp Ford, C.S.A.

names. No one would tell, no one dared to tell, for if any prisoner had told, he would not live long enough to tell any tale. So we got nothing to eat that day. That night we had a heavy rain which, of course, soured the meal. They gave us no rations of any kind the next day.

Towards evening one the Federal officers told a rebel officer that the boys were making preparations to break from the stockade, and attack the guard, for they would rather die a soldier's death in battle, than be starved to death. It was not more than a half an hour after this, that the mules were harnessed into the wagon and driven into camp. They were not long in issuing rations, each man got about half a pint of meal, all soaked and soured, ready to lay on a stone and bake. For my part, I was almost starved to death. Many is the time that I have been down behind the officer's cabins, looking for an old crust of bread which they would throw away, because they could not eat it, but I should have been glad of it, for the rations we got part of the time, would not have been enough, to keep a pair of chickens from starving, in this part of the country.

Disease, in all its worst forms was amongst us, some had the measles, others had the smallpox, fevers, chills, scurvy and Satan's itch.[13] I had the itch and scurvy in its worst form; whenever I laid down on the ground to rest (for the ground was our bed), I would have to clear all the pieces of wood or stone from under me, for if I lay on a small piece of wood, it would sink into my flesh, and leave a black spot. My flesh was all decayed, and I was fast failing. Proud flesh would start out

---

13 Satan's Itch or Hell's Itch is the result of a sunburn on one's shoulders and back that causes an excruciating, stabbing deep itch that comes in fiery un-scratchable waves that consume one with panic. "What the Heck is Hell's Itch?," *Cleveland Clinic HealthEssentials,* Jul. 11, 2018, https://health.clevelandclinic.org/what-the-heck-is-hells-itch/.

Quaters at Camp Ford Texas

Federhen's personal sketch of how his quarters looked at Camp Ford.

Federhen, first manuscript draft

of these spots, and was continually bleeding.[14] Flies were numerous, and very troublesome, for they would get into my flesh, and breed skippers.[15] These little pests would occupy my time a great deal. I have sat for hours picking out these pests with a stick. The itch along with the scurvy, body lice and head lice, kept me scratching and digging the most of my

14 Proud flesh, also called granulation tissue, is "the formation of a multicellular mass of tissue in response to an injury . . . (it) contains many new blood vessels and, in its later stages, large numbers of fibroblasts." *Oxford Concise Medical Dictionary,* 8th ed. (New York: Oxford University Press, 2014).

15 "Skipper" is a small maggot. *Oxford English Dictionary,* online edition, consulted 2018.

time; I was not the only one. The w
with these torments. I have seen men t
as I was, lie down and die. Their flesh a
bones by these skippers, for there was noth
us but bones.

There were a few iron pots in camp, which
messes had to boil their meat in, and they would s
lend one of these pots to other prisoners, to boil their
in. Whenever we got one of these pots, it was deemed a g
treat. Four of us would use it at a time, some would put
pants and shirt, others would put in their blanket, for they
had neither pants nor shirt to cover themselves. I had
nothing but a part of a pair of pants, which were considerably
worn out, and the bottoms of them just covered my knees.
These I would put to boil to kill the skippers, etc. I would have
to stop in the cabin until they got dry again, for I had nothing
else to wear. This was the case with a great many.

Some of the boys who had blankets, would cut them up
and make a pair of pants and a shirt, we had no needles,
thread, or sewing machine. The needles we had were made
out of a piece of bone, with a hole made in one end and
sharpened at the other end. For thread, we would pull an old
blanket to pieces, and unravel the yarn. This we would use
double, so that it was quite strong.[16]

These hardships and troubles were not severe enough for
the rebel commander, so he ordered that every prisoner
should be vaccinated. This, he said, would keep disease from
us. So the doctor commenced inserting poisonous matter into
the arms of nearly half the boys in camp.[17] This, of course,

---

16 In other words, the thread was run twice through the eye of the needle.

17 Standard vaccination practices in this period involved cutting the skin,
inserting a small amount of dried lymph from another infected person, and
then pressing the edges of the cut together so that the skin would heal over

became very sore and
arms were so offensive
.[18] A number lost their
is vaccination. It was a
ground, helpless, not
food, here they would
sease, with the itch,

ur were carried out of
a man died, he was
and hill, close to the
...however there was a heavy rain storm, the water would soak through this hill and run into the spring which supplies the camp with water. At times, the water was so bad on account of the dead bodies, that it was almost impossible to drink it, but we could get no other, so we were obliged to use that or none.

To add to my troubles, one day as I was blowing the fire with part of an old straw hat, to make it burn, a red-hot cinder flew from the fire and settled itself between my toes. My flesh being tender, it burnt through before I could remove it. It made bad work, and instead of eating my rations of meal that day, I made a poultice of it, and put it on my foot, but it did no good, it because full of proud flesh, and began to

---

the infectious matter. Glenna R. Schroeder-Lein, *The Encyclopedia of Civil War Medicine* (Armonk, NY: M.E. Sharpe, 2008), 320–21.

18 In this sense, mortification is localized necrosis of the tissue. This was "offensive" because of the rotting stench and repulsive sight. (*Oxford English Dictionary*). Such side effects were known to result from infections caused by poor hygiene in the vaccination process. Schroeder-Lein, *Encyclopedia of Civil War Medicine*, 321.

19 The prisoners' graves were near the northern corner of the stockade. Lawrence and Glover, *Camp Ford*, end papers.

spread from toe to toe. After this it began to mortify and soon my whole foot was as black as jet.

There was a stream of waste water, from the spring, which run across one corner inside of the stockade, in which the boys were in the habit of washing.[20] One day as I was washing my feet and limbs at this stream, a rebel doctor stopped and asked me how it happened. He examined my feet, and said I should have to lose it, and if it was not seen immediately, that I might lose my leg or life. He told me to wait at the gate until he went to head-quarters to get me a pass to go to the hospital. I watched him until he got out of sight, then I started to my cabin, there to remain for two days, so as not to be seen by the doctor, for I well knew that if he got me out of there, I should never see the stockade again, for there were very few who went there, that ever returned. We could see the pine boxes carried from the hospital to the hill, regular every day, besides what were carried from the stockade. It has been said by rebel leaders, that every Yankee that they captured and held as a prisoner, would never be able to do service in the army again.

There was a hill on the south side of the camp that covered nearly half an acre. This was not occupied by any huts or cabins, but was used expressly for a walking park, and prize-fighting ring, if any of the boys out of the different messes got to quarrelling about any simple matter, the rest of the boys would make them go to the ring, and fight it out. Fighting and stealing were the only amusements about that we had in camp. It was not very amusing to the party who stole or fought. When a man stole anything, and was found guilty, he had a very severe punishment. The party whom he had stolen from would notify the rest of the boys, then nearly all the camp would come together for the purpose of

20 Waste water was water in excess of the needs of the camp. *Oxford English Dictionary.*

witnessing his sentence. They would take him to the southwest corner of the stockade, where the sinks were dug about six feet deep and four feet wide, with legs laid from one side to the other.[21] Here they would take their prisoner and throw him in, then they would sink him, until his head was just above the surface. They would then let him remain to get out the best way he could; by the time he got out, he had no friend to comfort him or take him in their cabins to shelter him from the boys, who were throwing sticks and stones at him, and calling him pretty names. He would hide away in some hole in the ground, there to remain till dark, so as to go to the spring to wash himself, that he might not be seen by his comrades. This was fun for the rebel soldiers who were on guard at these times.

Ingenuity was in progress every day: chequers, chessmen and musical instruments of our own manufacture. These instruments consisted of tambourine, fiddle, banjo and clappers.[22] Some of the officers had some cats given to them by their rebel friends for pets, as soon as the kittens grew, the old cats were killed, their skin was cleaned and boiled so as to get the hair off, and then dried. These skins they would use to make tambourine and banjo heads. For banjo and fiddle strings, they would use some part of the cat's innards. There were some very handsome fiddles made in camp, perhaps not as fancy as those made in the Eastern states, for they have tools to work with, and the tool we had was either an old pocket or case knife.

The officers had very good times, pleasant nights, for they would get the band together, and have a dance, and after dancing, they would sing or have the band play. One dark

---

21 "Sink" means cesspool. "Legs" were supports upon which the men sat while relieving themselves. *Oxford English Dictionary.*

22 A clapper is a musical instrument that imitates the sound of hands clapping. *Oxford English Dictionary.*

night, the band was playing, and the men were singing very patriotic and comic songs, in a cabin near the center of the eastern side of the stockade. The camp was quiet, all but this cabin, and the Johnnies that were on guard were quite lonesome, so they left their post to stand as near as they could to the cabin, to hear the singing and the music. The rebs were very much amused and forgot the rain and their posts. One of the rebs would sing out for the boys to play Dixie. This they would do, and the Johnnies would join in the chorus. We were having a nice time, until the officer of the guard came around then to examine the different posts, when, to the surprise of the officer and guard, they found on the southeast corner of the stockade, two pickets had been removed, and by this, they knew that prisoners had been escaping, while the music was going in, and the guards had been most interested. The boys thought of the opportunity that afforded them an escape, so, while the boys were playing and singing the loudest, so as to keep the attention of the guard from the post, others were removing the pickets and making their escape. As soon as the rebs found it out, the boys stopped their music and everything was quiet for the rest of the night.

The next morning, the blood-hounds and mounted horsemen, were put on the trail of the escaping men. Twelve men escaped, and before noon, eight of them were brought back to the stockade. They looked very tired and hungry, and some of them were very badly bitten by the blood-hounds. The other four prisoners were never heard from but the rebs said that they let their hounds tear them to pieces, so as to get a taste of Yankee blood. Whenever a prisoner got away and was not recaptured, the rebs always brought back that sort of a report, so as to frighten us, so we would not attempt to escape, but the Yankees were not so easily frightened, they were always contriving some means of escape.

At last the rebel officers divided the camp into eight separate wards, each ward having its number of men. Ten men were detailed every day out of each ward to go out under guard to get wood to cook with. Men would sometimes escape from these squads, but were always brought back and punished. The rebel officers got tired of chasing men that ran away from their squad so every squad that went out, had to have a Federal officer go with them, to be responsible for the men. There were not many who escaped now, for the officers were very particular who they took with them. The rebs said, if any prisoner escaped out of the squads while the officer was with them, and was not recaptured, that the officer should be punished severely.

Now came the news that the U.S. Sanitary Commission had sent the prisoners clothing, and we were all looking for them every day and dreaming about them at night. At last they came. There were four wagon loads of large boxes drove into camp. These contained the clothing, and were left in charge of the officers in camp, to be distributed amongst the prisoners. Some of the boxes had been opened and the rebs had been helping themselves. The boxes contained all army clothing. There were pants, shirts, shoes, socks, blankets and underclothing. The clothes were distributed amongst the prisoners. The officers looking out that they had a good supply, before they issued any of the rest. I got a pair of pants, shoes and socks, and a blanket. I had not had the blanket but a few days, before it was stolen from me.

There was one case of medicines amongst the officers. This was the most important article for us, for the rebs, if they had any medicine, would not give it to a Yankee prisoner. There was also a doctor in camp, and he had charge of the medicines. Every morning he would have twenty or thirty men waiting their turn to see the doctor, and get some medicine. Some of them had the scurvy. Others had the itch. Some had the scurvy in the head, so that had lost all their teeth, and were losing their eyesight, besides becoming bald headed. After the doctor had seen all the patients at his office, he would go through the camp, to see after the sick men who were not able to leave their beds. Some he would find very badly off, some had the small pox, some the measles.

I have seen men, lying on the ground without any covering for their bodies, and only a little brush and leaves erected over them, to keep the dew from falling on them at night, for they had sold all their new clothes for something to eat, they not being able to cook their own food, here they would lie from morning till night, eat up by the small pox, and the flesh and even the ground around them, would be full of skippers and vermin.

I was a constant visitor to the doctor's office myself, for my flesh was all decayed, and my feet were hardly able to hold me up. The doctor's prescription was to drink wood ashes mixed in water, and keep meal poultice on my feet. He also put burnt alum on where there was any proud flesh, so as to burn it out.[23]

My feet began to improve, and so did I for a while, until the medicine gave out. The proud flesh had all been burnt out, but the sores will always remain as they were then. The scurvy was getting the best of me, and I knew that if I stopped there much longer, that I should share the fate of those of my comrades who had been buried on the hill.

23 This was probably aluminum potassium sulfate dodecahydrate ($KAl(SO_4)_2 \cdot 12H_2O$) that has been calcinated, or heated to high temperatures in open air. It was used to treat skin diseases. John Forbes, Alexander Tweedie, and John Conolly, eds., *The Cyclopædia of Practical Medicine* (Philadelphia: Blanchard and Lea, 1859), 485.

5

The Prisoners' Tunnel Is Discovered

THERE WERE not any of the prisoners escaping now, and I knew it was about time for me to try my luck in escaping for I had rather run the risk of being shot in trying to escape, than be left here to die from the horrid disease I had in my system.

We were still at work digging the tunnel; we had got it dug about one hundred and thirty feet long, and were thinking about opening it to make our escape, when it was discovered. The rebs had been trying to find out where it was, but could not. There was a prisoner in camp who had belonged to the rebel army, and had deserted to the Federal. He was afterwards recaptured by the rebels, but none of them knew him at the time of his recapture, and so he was put in with the rest of us as a Yankee.

One day as he was at the spring to get water, he was recognized by the rebel guard as a deserter from the army. He was reported at head-quarters and was soon put under arrest, and taken from the stockade. Everything was quiet that day, the boys and officers were all wondering what they took him for. The did not have to wait long to find out, for the next morning at roll call, the rebel officers and guard were all armed through the camp, ordering every man to fall into the ranks in their different wards, and remain there until the horn was blown. They showed no respect to the sick and dying, for they would have to be brought out of their cabins in blankets, and laid in the ranks, and as soon as the cabins were empty, the guards helped themselves to anything that was worth taking. Now that they had got all the Yankees into rank, the rebel officers came in with this deserter; he took them to the cabin where the tunnel was started from, and showed them how it was dug, and how far. Some of the rebs brought shovels in with them and now they went to digging, to find the entrance of the tunnel. After digging about five feet, they came to the boards that covered the entrance. They took the boards up and there found their prize. This was all they wanted, they cheered and shouted, and said that our Yankee tricks were played out.

I did not blame the deserter for exposing the secret, for I think I should have done the same thing had I been placed in his situation. His sentence was death for desertion, but the rebs promised him his freedom, if he would tell what was going on in camp, which he did.

The next thing was to find the men that were digging the tunnel. So the rebel officers with their man walked through the ranks, and marched out four of us as being the head of the diggers. After they had marched us out of the stockade, they blew the horn, and the rest of the prisoners went to their cabins, to see what was missing for the rebs had taken a great many things away with them. They marched us to the head-quarters of the rebel commander. He was a cross, ugly looking fellow, with a heart as big as a flea. As soon as we were in his presence, he began to curse and swear, and called us anything but gentlemen. He said if it were in his power, he would have every prisoner in the stockade shot, for he despised a Yankee. The adjutant took our names, the place we enlisted, and where we were captured. When I told him I was from Boston, Mass., he gave a groan and a look at me as if he would like to put me where I should never see daylight again, for they have no love for Massachusetts' men and call them negro thieves and abolitionists.

The officers began to ask questions, how we dug, what we dug with, and how we see to work underground; we told them that we dug it with a knife, and could see to dig in the dark as well as the light. After asking us a great many questions, they asked the commander what should be done with us. He ordered us to be set to work digging and filling the hole up again. The officer asked if he should get us shovels to dig with. He growled out,

"No, put two guards over them, and make them fill it up, the same way they dug it."

This was impossible, for the tunnel was six or seven feet underground, and by digging down through the earth that distance with a knife only, we could not gain more than one inch a day, for the earth was full of hard, red clay and sand stone.

The prisoners were all standing near the gate, and on the hill, looking at the rebel head-quarters, to see what became of us, when we came from the commander. The guard told the boys in camp that we were going to be shot. There was a great excitement at this. The rebels put on double guard around the stockade, for they were afraid the prisoners would make a break.

The guard set us a work digging, but it was slow work. We had dug but very little when it began to grow dark, and the guards told us to go to our cabins, and be there to work the next morning, as soon as it was light. The cabin from which the tunnel was started was cleaned of everything, and then the guards went away, cautioning us to be there early the next morning, without fail.

6

SECOND ATTEMPT
TO ESCAPE CAMP FORD

THAT NIGHT the four of us met to plan some way of escaping. We went to the cabin where the tunnel was to see if we could not push it through and escape that night. Everything was quiet, and the rebels had all gone to rest, except those on guard. These would call out every half hour. Each man would, as his pose was numbered, call the number of his post and the time of night. Thus, "Post number three, half past two o'clock and all is well." If a guard did not call, you would know that he was fast asleep or was off his post. Everything was in our favor, so we set to work.

The mouth of the tunnel was open, so one of the boys went in for the purpose of opening the other end. He stayed there about half an hour, when he came out and said that he had dug almost to the surface of the ground. It was my turn to go in next. I was to take everything along with me, that I wanted to carry. I had on my best clothes, and a haversack on my back, filled with a few pieces of dried corn bread and dried beef. The fellow that went in first was a much smaller person than myself, so he could get through a much smaller hole than myself. The first that he dug, he threw back into the tunnel, so that it made it much smaller. And I had to lay down and pull myself along by my hands. I had got almost to the end, when it got so small, that I could not pull myself through. I had the knife, and tried to dig my way, but found that it was of no use. The best thing that I could do was to turn, or rather push, myself back, so I commenced to push back, and the harder I pushed, the firmer I was wedged in, for my haversack had pushed itself over my back and was answering every purpose of a wedge.

There I was, five feet underground and about one hundred and twenty from the entrance, and could not move either way. My strength had nearly left me, for it was cold, damp and suffocating, for there was no chance of any air getting into the tunnel. The thoughts of death in this situation were enough to set me crazy.

After laying here a few moments, I made another effort. I breathed all the air out of my system, and then pushed myself back. This would have been the last effort, if I had not succeeded in releasing myself from my haversack. The haversack slipped over my head and I was again free. My blouse and shirt were torn off my back. I did not stop for the pieces, but pushed myself out of the tunnel as quickly as possible.

When I arrived at the mouth, I found the boys were getting ready to follow me, thinking I had made my escape. I was too weak to get out of the hole, so they took me out. I was almost too weak to talk. I told them it was of no use for them to try to make their escape through the tunnel, for they could not get through. I was covered with mud, and my back and breast were both bleeding, for they had been bruised when I had made my last effort to get out. The boys got some water, and washed the blood and mud off, so that I went to my cabin.

I did not sleep any that night. I was thinking what a narrow escape I had had from death, and I do not think I should have lived much longer, had it not been for the excitement of escaping which was always in my mind. I never mentioned it to my messmates, and never talking with them about escaping.

7

Successful Escape from Camp Ford

IN THE morning, one of the boys brought me a shirt to wear for mine, along with my haversack, was left in the tunnel. I put it on, and then turned out at roll call. After the roll call, the guard told me to be at the stockade in half an hour, ready to dig, he giving me just time enough to eat my breakfast.

I ate my little piece of corn bread in a hurry, and then went to the doctor's office. I asked him if he had any spirits of turpentine; he wanted to know what I wanted it for. I told him that I had been carrying wood on my back for several days, and that I wanted it to bath my back with. He said he would get me some, if there was any out at the hospital. So he went out to get it, and soon returned with a small bottle full. He wanted me to return the bottle as soon as I got through with it. I did not promise him that I would nor did I intend to. I went to the stockade, and went to work. The rebs had got us some shovels to dig with. We worked until noon, when the rebs gave us an hour for dinner, telling us to be sure and be back, as soon as our hour was up.

My dinner was ready for me, such as it was, as soon as I got to my cabin I ate it, and then went to work, washing and dressing my wounds, for they were always bleeding and not getting any better, but growing worse. I had the chronic diarrhea on me, so that I was not able to walk from my cabin to the hill. I had almost given up the idea of ever leaving the camp alive, after having been foiled in our last attempt.

While I was washing my wounds, the wood-squad was called together to go out after wood to burn. The thought struck me that I might disguise myself so as to go with them; so I went into the next cabin to see one of the boys who were going out, to see if I could not go in his place. I promised him half the wood I got if he would let me go, so he consented. I took a piece of corn bread, and a piece of dried meat, and put them in my pocket for lunch, and told one of the boys in my mess, that perhaps he would never see me again. I did not wait to answer any questions, but started down to the gate, for the wood squad were just going out. I had my cap down over my eyes, so that I passed the guard at the gate, and was not detected.

My hour was not quite up. It had about ten minutes to run. I knew that if I was going to make any escape, that I must be about it before my hour was up. There were but two guards when with us six, besides the officer. We went about half a mile from the stockade after the wood. I did not dare to go with a load of wood on my back to the stockade, so I would gather small pieces of dried wood, which lay about, and lay them in a pile, so as to make them think that I was very industrious. I would stray away a little further from the guard each time, until I got a good opportunity to get a large tree between them and myself. The guards were rather careless, so I watched the chance when they were busy talking, and not paying any attention to their duty, to get behind the tree. As soon as I had got the tree between them and myself, I started.

I was very weak, but excitement kept me up. I kept on in the northwest direction. I had not been gone more than half an hour, when I heard the bugle call at head-quarters. This was to call the blood-hounds and mounted men together. I well knew what it meant. I had expected it, for I had seen the same thing before. I did not lose any time thinking what to do, for as soon as I heard the howl of the hounds, and shouts of the men, I took the little bottle of spirits of turpentine from my

Hounds chasing escaping Union prisoners in Texas

Harper's Weekly, November 21, 1863

pocket, tore off a piece of my shirt to use as a sponge and bathe my feet and legs with it, pulled up my pants, and dropped what was left in the bottle on my trail, and then started on the run for life.[1]

I ran for about half a mile, through the woods, when I stopped and laid down not being able to go any further, and did not care much whether I was ever able to get up again or not, for I had got discouraged and disheartened at the thoughts of being run to death by these hounds. I had one consolation, however, and that was that I had got away from them, and that the dogs could not follow me any further.

I had not laid there but a few minutes when I heard loud talking and swearing and smashing through the timber for

1 Presumably, the odor of the turpentine would mask Federhen's personal scent and foil the tracking by the hounds.

when the dogs came up to where I put the turpentine on my feet they could not go any further, for it had killed the scent. They stayed there about half an hour, when their sounds died away, and I knew that they had gone.

I lay there until dark, then I got up and walked towards camp, until I came in sight of the hospital. There was a Kansas soldier here, who was playing off sick, and he told me that anytime I made my escape, to come to the hospital, and he would be ready to go with me. There was but one guard on post at the hospital and I knew it would be easy enough to get by him. So I waited until he got to the opposite side of the house, and then stole in.

I found my man sitting along with a lot more sick men around the fire. I spoke to him, and when he saw me, he was very much surprised, and begged me to leave the hospital, for he was afraid the hounds would trace me there. I told him how I escaped and got away from the brutes, so he was satisfied, and we prepared to start on our journey. There were two other men who wanted to join us. Both of them lived in the western part of Texas, and proposed starting towards where they lived.[2]

We all agreed to this, but the next thing was to get out of the hospital without being seen by the guard. It had been cloudy all day, and now it had begun to rain quite fast, and the air was very cold. The guard was stooping over a camp fire to get warm, when we stole out of an end window and started for the brush.

---

2 There were only four units of Texas men who fought with the U.S. Army. The 1st U.S. Cavalry and the 2nd U.S. Cavalry both served in Louisiana during 1864, and may have been the units to which these prisoners belonged. *Official Army Register of the Volunteer Force of the United States Army for the Years 1861, '62, '63, '64, '65*, Part IV: *Texas* (Washington, DC: Government Printing Office, 1865), 1647; Frank H. Smyrl, "Texans in the Union Army, 1861–1865," *Southwestern Historical Quarterly*, 65 (1961), 234–50.

There was a running stream of water at the foot of the hill just back of the hospital. We walked through the water, down the stream, for about a mile, so that in case they set the dogs after us, they could not find the trail. It was raining very fast, so that it made it very bad travelling, for we had to travel through the woods altogether. We travelled all night in a northwestern direction, taking our direction from the wind and rain.

As soon as it was daylight, we were afraid to travel any further, so we lay down in the brush for the day. We did not sleep much, for the excitement kept us awake. We planned the route we were to take. The two Texas boys were to guide the way. One was named Edwin Wallace and the other Joseph Brown. My companion was Rufus Custard.[3]

---

3 Wallace and Brown have not been identified, and no soldiers with those names are recorded in any Union-affiliated units from Texas during the Civil War. As later events imply, they may have been using aliases. An Edwin Wallace (b. 1848, d. 1923) served in Company D of the Frontier Battalion, Texas Rangers, during the Indian Wars. At the time of his death, he was a resident of Grayson County, the seat of which is Sherman. Rufus Custard was born in 1831 in Pennsylvania (perhaps Springfield), and by 1860 had settled in Bourbon County, Kansas, which is on the border of Missouri. He died in Bourbon County in Aug. 1884. See, 1850 Federal Census, 1865 Kansas State Census, and U.S. Find a Grave Index, all of which are available at www.ancestry.com.

8

WALKING ACROSS TEXAS

(PERHAPS AUTUMN 1864)

WE WERE to go to Wallace's house first, to get rations, for all the rations we had were about a dozen ears of corn. Night came on, and the stars shone brightly, so that we could easily get the right direction.

We travelled night after night through woods and swamps, not daring to come in sight of any house, and made sure to keep a safe distance from any village. We had travelled some three hundred miles[1], and I had begun to feel quite smart. My diseases were all getting better, but my clothes were getting the worse for wear. We were about out of rations, and would have to live on wild onions and sassafras roots. These made a very good meal for a change.

We had about one hundred miles further to go before we should come to Wallace's house. I had noticed for one or two nights, that Wallace and Brown had a great deal to say in private to each other, but never suspected they were going to give us the slip, but it proved so the next night. We had been travelling through a long piece of woods, when we came to a small river, and beyond the river, on a hill, was a log cabin. None of us knew exactly where, or in what part of the country we were. So two of us were to go to the house and inquire the

1 Sherman, mentioned below, is about 130 miles from Camp Ford.

direction to the town of Sherman, and as soon as they found out, to come back and report. Wallace and Brown said that they would go, and off they started.

We crossed the river, Custard and myself stopping at the foot of the hill to wait for the other two to return. I watched the house, but could see no light. We waited about half an hour, and they did not return. I told Custard that I reckoned they had given us the slip, but he could not believe it, so we waited a little longer, but they did not come. I proposed going to the house to see if we could see them. I went up to the house and knocked, and a voice from inside, enquired, "Who's there?" I could not think for an instant what to say, but Custard spoke up and said, "Two Confederate soldiers from Camp Ford, in search of some Yankee prisoners, who made their escape."

The old man got out of bed and let us in the house. We were cold and hungry, and, worst of all, our guides had left us. Custard was a better talker than myself, so I let him do the talking. The old man's wife, lay in some straw at one end of the cabin, asleep. I told him that we were hungry, and asked him if he would give us something to eat. He awoke his wife, who got up. The fire was kindled, and soon the corn meal was baking before it. We all sat around the fire, talking about the war, and how destitute the country was. The old man talked more like a Yankee than a rebel, and soon he told us that he was a Union man, and that he did not care who knew it.

After we had eaten supper, we all sat down around the fire to have another chat. While we were talking, the old man asked us how it was that we were unarmed, if we were in this part of the country trying to recapture runaway Yankees. He said he reckoned we're the runaways, and that he was very glad to see us. We then told him who we were, and how we happened to be there. He gave us some good advice. He told us who the Union men were on our route, and filled our pockets with corn bread. When we started, he came to the door, and pointed out the direction to Wallace's house. He said it was about one hundred miles further, and that it was very bad travelling, for most of the way, we should have to travel through swamps, and woods, and cross some large rivers. One of them was the Sabine, and the other the Trinity.[2] Between these rivers, was nothing but wild brush and swamps, full of thorns and briars. We thanked the man for his kindness and started once more on our journey, alone, to travel by night through the woods and swamps, and lay in the brush during the day.

We had travelled about fifty miles, and had crossed the Sabine, when we came to the Trinity River bottom, or swamp. The people in that part of the country call it a river bottom, because when the river is high, it overflows its banks, and extends for miles, so that it is impossible for any animal to pass through it. It began to rain the first of the evening, and this did not add any to our progress, for it was almost impossible for us to travel through it. Every step we took, our feet would sink into the soft clay, and there was so much suction in it, that it was all we could do to pull one foot before the other. Sometimes we would crawl along on a fallen tree, and very often the limbs would break and let us down in the mud and briars. We travelled this way until about midnight, when we came to the Trinity River.[3]

It was frightful to see and hear the river. It was roaring and foaming at a great rate, and sounded more like a large pack of wolves, than anything I can compare it to. We kept

2 At its closest, the Sabine River is about 16 miles north of Camp Ford and 100 miles southeast of Sherman. It flows east and then south to the Gulf of Mexico and forms part of the boundary between Texas and Louisiana. The headwaters of the Trinity River are about 60 miles due west from Sherman but the river takes a southward bend about 33 miles west of Sherman. It flows south-southeastward into Galveston Bay.

3 Depending on the direction traveled after crossing the Sabine, this may have been more than 100 miles, or as few as 70 miles.

along the banks of the river, hoping to find a bridge, but all the bridges had been washed away, and I began to feel as if I should like to be washed away too, for I was getting disheartened and tired of life. I had not slept any, since our guides had left us, so that weariness was overpowering me. It was getting to be near morning, but the rain had not abated.

It thundered, lightened and rained still harder. I proposed to Custard to go back and give ourselves up to the first town we should come to, so we might be carried back to the stockade. He said he was willing, so we left the river and soon we came to a high piece of land. It was a little better walking here. We had not traveled far, when I began to feel as if I was paralyzed and wanted to go to sleep. I can't describe the feeling as I had it and I made it known to my partner. I lay down on the soft bed of mud and fell fast asleep. He let me sleep for half an hour and then awoke me. I wanted to go to sleep again, but he would not let me. He said that I was too weak to sleep long at a time.

We traveled through brush and briars all the morning. About noon we came to a road, along which we traveled in the direction of the stockade, hoping that by some chance some scouts might pass and pick us up. I had not walked a great way before I fell to the ground asleep. I do not know how long I lay there, but when Custard awoke me, it was quite dark. I did not feel able to get up or walk, so I told him to go ahead and get back to camp as soon as he could, and let me stay where I was, but he said he would not do anything of the kind. He rubbed my limbs, and gave me some water, and then helped me to get up, and then, on we went.

We had not traveled more than a mile, when we saw a light in a window, some way ahead of us. This gave us some encouragement, and we were both eager to get to the house. When we were within a few rods of the house, we stopped to wash ourselves in a mud hole, so as to look nice and slick before we went in. While I was washing myself, I fell into the mud asleep. My partner picked me up, and helped me to wash the mud off my face and clothes. We went up to the house, and knocked on the door. The old lady came, and let us in. Custard told her that we were Confederate soldiers, going home on sick leave. There was a bright fire burning on the hearth, so the old lady sat us beside it to dry our clothes. I had no sooner sat down, than I was over on the floor. The fall awoke me, but I was so near dead, that I did not have strength enough left to get up alone.

The lady took pity on me and made up a bed of straw in one corner of the room where I lay down. They kept me there two days, not expecting me to live from one day to the other. This rest did me a great deal of good, and I felt quite smart. Custard proposed to go to Wallace's house, and get rested, and get some provisions. The weather was clear and the roads quite dry, so that we could travel quite easy.

We did not travel much that night, for we were both thinking how it would do to travel in the daytime along the roads, and call ourselves Confederate soldiers on parole. This plan worked very well, for we stopped at houses along the road, and when we felt hungry we would beg for something to eat, telling them that we were Confederate soldiers on our way home in Kansas, and they were always ready to give something to a soldier. Nights we had a bed to sleep on, or rather the floor, for most of them lay on some straw on the floor.

One night we stopped at a house. It was quite late and the folks had gone to bed, so I knocked at the door and a woman came and wanted to know who we were. I told her we were soldiers on parole, and had traveled a great many miles that day, and wanted lodging for the night. She said she had no room for us, unless we lay on the floor before the fire. I told her that would do, and so we went in. The house was about eighteen feet square. By the light of the fire, I could see four persons (I could not tell whether they were men or woman) laying in one corner of the room asleep, so we lay down on the floor, with our feet before the fire, and were soon fast asleep.

I had not slept long, before I was awakened by something or somebody stepping over me. I started to jump to my feet, when I found that something like a log lay across my body. It frightened me at first, but as soon as I began to kick, it began to grunt and make a noise. My partner awoke, and began to kick also, and between us both we succeeded to kicking him into the fire. It was a large hog, and as soon as he touched the fire, he set up an awful groaning and grunting, which awoke everyone in the house. The woman who let us in got up and patted the hog on the head, and called him her pet hog and then took him into bed with her.

We did not hear anything of the pet pig that night and I lay there thinking to myself what kind of women they were. In the morning when we awoke, the woman had breakfast ready for us, and we sat down to the table. Our coffee was made of corn meal burnt, and it tasted as much like coffee, as anything could, and not be coffee. No milk, no sugar, no butter on our corn cakes, and no plates to eat from. The knives were worn within two inches of the handles, and the forks were made of wood. Notwithstanding all these inconveniences, we began to eat. The women had so much to say about their husbands in the army, that we talked more than we ate. After breakfast, we thanked the women for their kindness, and started along the road to walk by daylight the rest of the way.

Towards evening, we came in sight of a small town, the name of which I do not remember. As we were passing through the town, and had not met anyone who took any notice of us, we thought we were all right and hoped we should get out of sight of any scouts. We had got out of the town, and were passing through a thick piece of woods, when we heard horsemen after us. As soon as they came in sight, they drew their revolvers and commanded us to halt. They rode up to us and asked us to what command we belonged. Custard told them that we were paroled soldiers from Gen. Lane's division in La., and that we were going to our homes in Kansas to get recruited.

They did not seem to be very inquisitive as to where we came from, but asked us if we had any money. We told them that we had none, but they did not believe us, so they dismounted, and one of them went through our pockets, while the other kept his revolver levelled at us, and said he would shoot us if we made any resistance. They could not find anything in our pockets, so they began examining our clothing, to see if we had on any better clothes than they had, for their' s were well worn out like our own. They condemned my clothes, but Custard had on a good pair of pants, and so they made him pull them off. After this they drove us off the road about a mile into the words, saying they were going to shoot us after they had got us out of hearing of the town. Soon we came to a river, and the rebs told us the best thing that we could do, was to jump in and drown ourselves. Here the rebs left us, and said that if we ever showed our heads out of the woods again, that they would blow us in pieces.

Here we were alone, and my partner without a pair of pants, and not being used to this kind of treatment, we were both of us quite disheartened. It was growing quite dark, and the night was cold. Both of us would willingly have been shot to put us out of our sufferings. What to do, we did not know. We were afraid that if we went back to the town, some of the scouts would see us, and it would go hard with us. So we concluded to stop in the woods, and travel as near to the road as possible, until we came in sight of a house.

We had not traveled long, before we came to a log cabin, set back some distance from the road. Custard stayed in the brush, while I went to the cabin to see what could be done for us. I went to the door and knocked, an old, pleasant grey haired man let me in. The inside of the cabin resembled the one of which I had been proprietor of in Camp Ford. There was only room enough for the old man and his wife. A bed took up one side of the room, and two chairs, and a table was the only furniture that they could get into their house conveniently. The old lady gave me her chair, and I sat down to tell them my story, when a faintness came over me, and I fell to the floor. A plenty of cold water, and a dose of whiskey, soon brought me to my senses, and I found myself lying on the bed. I set up on the edge of the bed. The old man wanted to know where I was from. I told him that I and another soldier had been discharged from the service on account of sickness, and that we were trying to get to our homes in Kansas, and that we had been robbed of all we had, and my friend was minus his pants, and that he could not go any further until I could get him a pair of old pants to wear. The old man and woman pitied us, and he got an old pair of pants, and told me to get my partner, and have him come into the house. I took the pants with me, and found Custard shivering with the cold, as if he would shake himself to pieces. He was so cold and numbed, that he could hardly speak. I helped him to put on the pants, and helped him to the house. The old lady had built us a hot fire and prepared us something. We ate with a good relish, and after we had got through, the old man began talking about the war.

He said what cussed fools the Yankees were to think that they could ever whip the Confederates. He despised the Yankees, and hoped that his two sons who were in the service would bring home the hearts of every Yankee that they shot. He only wished that he was young. He said that Washington, the Yankee's capital, was in possession of the confederates and that the whole of the Yankee army was demoralized. I listened with great interest to what the old gent said, and as I agreed with him in everything he did not know that he was talking to a federal soldier.

It has grown quite dark, and I proposed starting, the old man objected, and said that he would take the chairs and table out of the room, so that we could sleep on the floor, I thanked him for his kindness but thought that we had better start and travel a few miles, because we wanted to get home as soon as possible. So the old man and woman bade us good bye and off we started. As we were going out of the yard, I saw a horse blanket hanging on the fence, which he had forgotten to take in. As we went past it, I took it from its place and put it under my arm without the owner seeing me. This was just what we wanted, for our clothes were very thin and the nights were very cold, and we had nothing to cover us with.

We took the road and traveled about two miles, when we came to a house on the edge of the prairie. As we were passing the house, a man came to the door and asked us where we were going. I told him we were going home in Kansas, and I asked him if we were on the right road. He said that we were, but he thought it would be impossible for us to cross the prairie that night, and that we had better stop with him overnight. We went up to the door, and as I look in, I saw four men sitting around the fire, and I thought it was best not to go in, so I told him I reckoned I could find my way, and that the more we traveled, the sooner we would get home, and so we started again.

It was quite dark, and the first house that we would come to was about three miles distant. We travelled about a mile, when we saw a light in a house. It looked as if it was only a short distance, so we hurried towards it, and, after we had travelled about an hour, it looked about as near as it had before, but on we trudged hoping to reach it before the people retired for the night.

The prairie was lonesome, for there were no cattle or horses to be seen, and we could hear nothing but the howling of wolves in the distance, and rapidly growing nearer. I knew the wolves would get our scent very soon, and I looked around for a tree, but there were no trees, not even a bush to be seen. I did not know the nature of these wolves, so we both started on the run towards the house. We got within half a mile of the house, when they overtook us. Custard nor myself could speak a word, both of us expecting to be devoured by hungry beasts. We kept them at bay by swinging our canes in front of us and walking backwards towards the house; occasionally the cane would strike the foremost one on the head, and the Lord only knows what kept these animals from tearing us to pieces. We had reached the gate of the garden, and the house sat about twenty feet back from the fence. As we opened the gate, Custard shouted, "A friend, open your doors."

The call was instantly complied with and I pushed the gate too, so as to get the start of them, before they could get over the fence. We started on the run and shut the door behind us. We had no sooner got the door closed, before the whole fence was pushed down, and a large pack of wolves surrounded the house, howling, barking and snuffing at the doors. The doors were closed and barred, and the windows fastened, so that no admission could be made, I told the inmate who we were, and that we were Confederates, going home. The did not ask us many questions that night, for they saw that we were tired and wanted rest, so they made up a bed on the floor for us. We soon occupied it and were fast asleep. The wolves kept up their noise all night, but in the morning when we got up and looked out of the door, there was not one to be seen. The fence was all done, and the ground looked as if it had been plowed.

Breakfast was prepared, and after we had eaten our corn bread, and drank some of Dixie coffee, we felt quite refreshed. The man wanted us to stop with him that day and help him, so we went to work and built a fence, and helped him to sow the corn, after the work was all done we went out into the barn and slept the rest of the day.

After supper we sat and talked about the war, and Custard sang a few songs, we all went to bed early and slept until about midnight, when the wolves came about the house, and set up a frightful howling. They did not come into the yard, but stayed outside about an hour, and then went off, and we heard nothing more of them that night, in the morning after breakfast, we took our leave, and bade the folks goodbye. We travelled in the western direction toward Wallace's house. Two days and nights travelling, we would reach it, so we travelled across the prairie all day and part of the night, when we came to a river, the river was too deep to ford so we got two logs and put them together into the river. We then undressed ourselves and laid out clothes on the logs to keep dry, and then pushed off. I could not swim so I kept hold of the logs and kicked. We got across safe, and dressed.

There was a great many cattle on this side of the river, and things looked quite cheerful. We had not gone a great way, when we came to a prairie. We were tired, and felt if we had a little sleep, it would do us much good. So we lay down on the grass and were soon fast asleep. We slept all the rest of the night, and I do not know how much longer we would have slept, had I not been awakened by something blowing in my face. I opened my eyes and there stood a lot of cattle around us, one of them smelling and blowing in my face. I started, for at first I was frightened and I awoke my partner, and we frightened them off. It was a fine clear morning and the prairie did look handsome covered with horses and cattle, and not a tree or bush to be seen.

We travelled all day, not meeting any person or passing any house. The sun was about setting when we changed our course toward a piece of woods at a good distance off; as we came near to it we heard a dog bark and I knew that there was a house near. We hurried on; before dark we reached the woods, and struck a road; we passed several houses, and stopped at a small house, and asked for lodging. We were asked in, and there was an old man, his wife and two children. We told them that we were soldiers going home, and that we were going to call on an old friend, Mr. Wallace who lived in Dallas County.[4] He said that he had no spare beds, but he would make a bed on the floor if that would do. I thanked him and said that would do.

---

4 Dallas County surrounds the city of Dallas.

Before going to bed, Custard sang a few songs, which amused the children very much. The bed was made and we laid down, and were soon fast asleep. We slept sound all night, and in the morning after breakfast, we bade them good bye, and started along toward Wallace's house.

9

ENCOUNTERS WITH CIVILIANS IN DALLAS COUNTY

(PERHAPS AUTUMN 1864)

WE REACHED there about noon. We found the old man in the field in front of the house.

I spoke to him and asked him if his son had been here. He seemed quite confused, and said he had not been there, and did not know where he was. I told him that we were Union prisoners, and had escaped from Camp Ford. The old man looked at us from head to foot and wanted to know what business we had to come to his house. He told us that we had better clear out and travel toward Mexico or the scouts would capture us and that would be an end to us. I thanked him for the reception he gave us, and told him that if ever we were captured that he would hear from us in a different form, for I well knew in my own mind that Wallace and Brown had been there and the old man was telling a strong story.

We turned to leave, but the old man called us back, and asked us into the house. He gave us two little pieces of hard cornbread, and two ears of corn saying the he hoped we would not say anything about him if we were captured. He said that the scouts were watching him every day for they knew that he had a son in the Yankee army. He did not want us to stay there any longer. So without bidding him goodbye we left the house, and started in the direction for Mexico.

We had traveled about thirty miles when we met three confederate soldiers mounted and well armed. As we went past them they asked us where we were going. I told them that we were going to Mexico. They said that we were very foolish for trying to go for they had tried to, and had to turn back, for they would have to travel three days without water, and going across the prairie was very hot and the sand would blister our feet so that we could not travel. I thanked them and they rode on.

Discouraged and almost dead from weakness and hunger, I prayed that I might die or that some wild animal might spring from the woods and devour us to put an end to our misery. But this was not our fate. Custard asked me what we had better do. I did not know – only to try and find out where or in what direction Brown lived, so that we might try his folks, and see if we could not get some rations, and find out the right course to travel to get into the Federal lines. So we traveled back in the same direction that we had come until it was dark. We were very tired, so we went off into the woods, and lay down on the ground and fell asleep. We were awakened several times during the night by owls screaming and flapping their wings over our heads, but then we had no trouble in frightening them away. We layed there until daylight, and then started to find Brown's house.

We traveled that day until about the middle of the afternoon, when we found the widow Brown, an old lady, her invalid son and his wife asked us into the house and I told them that we were Confederate soldiers and had been guarding the Yankee prisoners at Camp Ford, and that her son John wished us to call at his house on our way home, and see his mother and let her know that he was well and expected to be exchanged soon. The folks seemed very glad to see us, and asked us to stay overnight. I knew all the evening by their talk that her son and Wallace had been there and that she had suspicion of us as being Federal prisoners. They asked us if there was many prisoners escaping from the stockade now. I told her that a great many tried to make their escape, but were always caught, and brought back or shot by the soldiers who captured them. I told her that it was a very hard matter for a prisoner to escape, for as soon as we found it out, the dogs were set on their trail and were soon recaptured. The old lady said she hoped that her son would never try to run away. We talked about the war, until it was quite late, and then went to bed.

In the morning after breakfast, Custard went out and I did not see anything more of him until evening. I felt quite uneasy about him for I feared he had been picked up by some scouts. He told the folks that he had been to see about joining the home guards in Dallas County.[1] I did not ask him any questions that night for he said that he was tired and wanted to sleep. The next morning we got up early and went out. He said he was going to see an old lady about a mile up the road to get her to bake a few Johnnycakes,[2] and then we would start the next morning. After we had called on the lady, we went back to the widow Brown's and got breakfast.

After we had eaten, Custard went off and said he would be back soon. I waited until noon, and then went out to find him. I went to the house where we had been in the morning, and asked the old lady if she had seen my friend since morning. She said that she had not, and so I went back again to the house. As I went in they told me that my friend had been there and had taken all the baggage and bade them goodbye saying that I was outside and that we were going to start for home. I told them that I had not seen him and I supposed that he had given me the slip. They felt very sorry, and asked me what I was going to do. I hardly knew what to do unless it was

---

1 The home guard was a volunteer militia for local defense. Wright, *Language of the Civil War*, 147.

2 Johnnycake is a type of cornbread made from cornmeal mixed with milk or water. Bartlett, *Dictionary of Americanisms*, 221.

to go into the woods and put an end to my sufferings, but something gave me strength and told me to keep on and never give up. I told the old lady that I was going out to join some scouting party if I could find any, and perhaps she would never see me again. So I bade her goodbye and started off without anything to eat and not knowing where I should get any.

I traveled round the rest of the day not meeting, or seeing a person. That night I lay in the woods and slept. My mind was wandering so that I did not rest much; in the morning it began to rain very hard, and I was chilled so that my teeth chattered, and I could not keep them still. I was very hungry and all I could get to eat was to pull the bark off the small trees and eat that. This was rather a poor substitute for food, but it was better than nothing.

I walked about all day long and slept in the woods that night. In the morning I got up and could hardly move I was so stiff with the cold. I walked along the road and soon came to a house. I knocked at the door, and an old man let me in. I inquired the way to widow Brown's house and he told me that I was about five miles from her house and if I would come in and wait a little while he would give me a ride a part of the way, for he was going within about a mile of her house with his horse and wagon and that he would like to have company; while he was getting his horse ready, his wife got me something to eat. I ate all she lay before me, and could have eaten more if she had given it to me, but she said that it was all she had, and her husband was going after some more meal, for they were all out. The old man had driven up to the door and I jumped into the wagon, and we both rode off. When we arrived at the nearest point to Brown's house, he showed me in what direction to go to get there. I thanked him and started off. I reached the widow Brown's about noon. They were surprised to see me and I knew that I was not welcomed but it did not make any difference to me. I went in and sat down to dinner.

After dinner the old lady told me that she could not have me stop there any longer for they were poor and had hard work to get enough to eat for themselves. I told her that I was perfectly satisfied but that I should not trouble her but a day longer for I was about to join the Home Guard. She did not believe any such thing and said that if I did not up and get away from the house that she or her son would go and report me to the military headquarters as being a Yankee. I said that would not trouble me in the least for it was just what I wanted. Her son who had been very busy during our conversation poking the fire with a stick of wood turned around and came towards me with the stick in his hand telling me that if I did not get out he would put me out. I thanked him and told him that he need not put himself to any such trouble. I saw that he was getting angry and that the stick began to shake. As he came nearer to me I arose and put my hand into my breast as if to secure some weapon, telling him that if he wanted to kick up a rumpus that I was ready for him. He said the he did not want to make any trouble only for me to leave the house. I then told him to keep his seat for I had something to tell him and his mother. He went back to his seat and wanted to know what I had to say.

So I told my story from the time I left Camp Ford to my arrival here and the mean trick that her son and Wallace had served us. They did not seem to know anything about it and when I told them then I was told by one of their neighbors that her son and Wallace had been here, she tried to deny it and said that she reckoned that I must be mistaken. I gave them to understand that I was not and if they wanted to put me out of the house I had no objections in going. I thanked her for the hospitalities given me during my unwelcome stay and asked her permission to stay one night longer, and in the morning I should leave and that they would not be apt to hear from me again.

The old lady and her son put their heads together for a few moments so I could not hear what they had to say. I saw they were uneasy, and that I had the best of them. After they had done talking, the son started towards the door and asked me if I did not want to take a walk in the garden. While we were walking and talking, he wanted me to promise him that I would not expose or say a word to any person or soldier that I had been at his house or that his brother or Wallace had been there. For if the military knew of it they would all of them be put to death. He also told me of several families that had been taken out of their houses in the night for expressing Union sentiments and hung in front of their own houses. He then told me that the first day Custard and myself came to the house that his mother told him we were Yankees and she wanted to get rid of us as soon as possible for fear the scouts would find us there and that would be sure to convict them.

Finding it was getting quite late I told him if he would give me something to eat and let me sleep in the house that night, in the morning I would leave the house and would say nothing to anybody about him, or that I had been at his house. He consented to this and we both went into the house and had our supper. After we had done we sat and talked about the war until quite late and then parted.

10

FURTHER TRAVELS IN TEXAS

EARLY IN the morning I arose before the rest were awake and started in a northwesterly direction not knowing or caring where I brought up.

I traveled all that day in the scorching hot sun, seeing nothing but wild horses and cattle. At night I reached a swamp and lay down on the branches of some fallen tree which lay together so as to make a comfortable bed, and there lay and slept until morning. As soon as I awoke, I prepared to wash myself in a mud hole; that was the best water I could get to wash in or to drink, for the river was about five miles away.

For breakfast I did not have a good hot cup of coffee and hot rolls nor for dinner did I have roast beef, for the morning I stole two ears of corn which was all the food I could get. I would not eat but a few kernels at a time for I did not know when I should get any more. I traveled all that day through the swamp not reaching any opening that would give me hope or any signs of the river. Occasionally I would come to a small opening where I could see blue sky. Here I would stop and rest. When I walked across the ground in these openings, the ground in front of me would rise and fall as it does on the ocean.

I traveled until it was quite late and then lay down on some fallen trees and went asleep. I do not know how long I slept but I was awakened by rain spattering in my face. The rain was increasing and it began to thunder and lightning. There came one peel of thunder that made the ground shake and I thought every tree in the swamp would fall. I crept under some fallen trees so as to protect myself from the rain. I lay in the water until it got so deep that I was obliged to get on some logs, for the water seemed to be coming out of the ground. Here I sat not knowing whether to turn back or to push forward towards the river. I sat here until morning.

The rain had ceased but the wind blew cold from the North making my situation very uncomfortable. What few clothes I had on my back were wet and stiff with the cold. I got down from the tree and found that the water was about two feet deep. This looked, I thought, rather discouraging but I kept on in the northern direction hoping to come to dry land, but the further I went the thicker the mire was. I could just hear the roaring of the river in the distance. I kept on, the water up to my knees and occasionally falling into a mud hole. This only increased my ambition to go ahead. I travelled all that day without coming in sight of dry land. I had eaten one ear of my corn, and the other had got quite soft from being wet.

It was getting quite dark and the owls began to scream and the frogs began their mournful sound. I was tired and worn out. It began to rain again so I laid down on some fallen trees and fell asleep. I was awakened a great many times by the owls screaming over me. I lay unto morning and then started for the river hoping that I might find dry land on the other side. I reached the river about noon. It was roaring at a fearful rate and to cross it would be impossible for man or beast. The opposite banks showed no more signs of dry land than where I was. What was I to do? My rations were very near exhausted and if I did not get out of the swamp before long, I should have to live on what I could get. Sassafras root grew in great abundance and that with a few onions made me a very good meal.

I stood looking at the river when suddenly I heard a crash. I looked up the river in the direction from which the sound came but could see nothing for the moment, when like a flash of lightening the current swept around a curve in the river about a quarter of a mile from where I was standing, carrying with it fallen trees and brush and seemed to sweep the banks as it roared and thundered through the woods. The next thought was to look to my own safety. I was standing with water then over my knees which did not make my situation any more agreeable. I started as fast as I could away from the river and took my course again in a northern direction. I traveled that afternoon and evening when I came out on higher ground, poling my way along not knowing where I was going or caring less.

Traveling this way half of the night I suddenly brought up against a fence; I could not see any house or shed so I laid down on some rails close to the fence and slept until morning. It had stopped raining but the weather was cold and cloudy and every thought of ever seeing home and friends again was driven from my mind, and not caring much of what became of me.

11

Captured by Confederates Again

Strolling along the fence through a piece of woods I came to a house. The most respectable looking mansion I had seen since I left Camp Ford. I approached the gate and a large hound greeted me with a growl which sounded to me as it came through his ivory teeth that he knew that I was a Yankee and he wanted me to look sharp.

As I neared the gate a young man came to the door, and wanted to know what I wanted. I told him that I was hungry and wanted something to eat. He asked me in and while going through the yard the hound kept close to my heels smelling and snuffing, and I was glad to get into the house out of his way.

I was soon provided for, and after a hearty breakfast of corn bread and bacon I was asked into another room where sat an old lady and gentleman and a young lady, the wife of the young man who proved to be a Confederate officer.

They asked me where I was from. I told them I was from Camp Ford, a Union prisoner. The old man arose from his chair with astonishment and wanted to know how in the thunder I came way out in this part of the country, and for what purpose and do you reckon you can travel in this part of the country without being found out? How many more of you are there around here? We will learn you Yankees better than to come in our country thinking you can whip we'ens.[1]

I was sitting on a stool near the door. The old man pacing the floor like a mad man muttering to himself and saying that he would fix me before the sun went down. I listened to the old man with great interest, and whenever I went to speak, he would stop me by saying the least I had to say the better it would be for me. I got up and started for the door but I was met in the doorway by the rebel officer who had his revolver in his hand telling me to go back or he would blow my brains out. Not being desirous of having my life taken just then, I retreated to the back part of the room and sat down.

I told him I was a paroled prisoner on my way home in Kansas and that he had no business to stop me on my journey. He wanted me to show my papers. I told him that I had lost them in the swamp with other papers and money and was not able to find them. He wanted to know if any other prisoners were paroled at the same time and how many. I told him there were six but they went by the way of Gransport.[2] He wanted to know if I was acquainted in Texas and if I had stopped at any house along the road. I said I had stopped to get something to eat and slept in the woods at night. He did not seem wholly satisfied with this and added that a scouting party was in the town about a mile distant and it was his duty to give me up to them. He laid his revolver on a small table close to the door and started to go out. As he turned his head, I hurried towards the table to get possession of the revolver but the old man got it before me and had it pointed towards

---

1 "We'ens" is usually rendered "we'uns" and serves in some Southern varieties of English as the first person plural pronoun. *Oxford English Dictionary.*

2 It is unclear which town Federhen is referring to. There is not a Gransport or Grandport in Texas. However, he may have meant Grandview, which is about 50 miles southwest of Dallas.

me, and I was obliged to get back. He said I could not play that but once and if I attempted to get up again, I was a dead man.

So there I was forced to set until the Rebel Officer returned and brought with him eight mounted men, and they were hard looking specimens of men. As I came out of the house, they all greeted me by crying out, hallow Yank; how do you do, Yank; nice man, Yank; any more Yanks around here; fetch them out, them's the fellows we like to deal with. I was not surprised at this talk for I had heard the same at Camp Ford, but if a Corporal's guard had showed themselves from the Union Army at that time, the Rebs would have scattered like sheep.

I did not fancy my situation in the least, but made up my mind to make the best of it, and get away from them as soon as an opportunity offered itself. As I approached them they gathered around me and began asking me questions. My answers to their many questions did not seem to please them and so they formed four riding in front of me and the other four in the rear. The Rebel Officer who was a Lieut. and went by the name of Lieut. Green accompanied us.[3] I did not like his looks from the first time I saw him. He had but one eye and that had a villainous look about it.

They marched me the rest of that day in the hot sun; at sunset they stopped on the edge of a prairie to camp for the night. They made a fire and began to cook some bacon and take some corn cakes from their haversacks. They kept a close watch over me and said if I attempted to run away they would riddle my body with bullets. I promised them I would not, hoping by this that they would give me some supper after

---

3 Junior 2Lt. L. D. Greene (also recorded at L. D. Green) served in Company C, Bourland's Regiment, Texas Cavalry. National Park Service, "Soldiers and Sailors Database," www.nps.gov/civilwar/soldiers-and-sailors-database.htm.

they had done. But instead of giving poor Yank his supper they put the leavings into their haversacks and said that that would do for their breakfast. I was hungry enough to eat shoe leather if I had a spare shoe. After supper they wanted to smoke and have a chat and thinking I was safer tied than at liberty. They took a rope from a saddle and tied my hands behind me and then tied me to a tree, and asked me if I wanted something to eat. I told then I did but all the answer I got was, "Then, get it if you can."

Tired and hungry as I was, I layed up against the tree so as to make my situation as comfortable as possible, while they had the chat. I overheard some of their conversation and one of them proposed to make a target shot of my head, but Lieut, Green said not, for he knew I was not in that part of the country for any good and he would make me tell before morning or he would bury my carcass at the foot of the tree.

Here they kept me until it was quite late and they were ready to turn in. They then released me and I lay on the ground between two of the guards some distance from the others. The Lieut. had some whispering to do to the two guards before they lay down and they both had very little to say to me. I did not sleep for my mind was too much occupied with thoughts of what was to come. I had laid about two hours and everything was quiet when I saw a man approaching us in the dark. It was the Lieut. He spoke to the guard and said he was ready. Green had a revolver in his hand and told the guard to bring Yank along with them. They traveled through the woods about half a mile and not a word was spoken, when they came out on a small open space.

Here they halted and I stood face to face with the three rebs. What was to come next ran through my mind. They have me in their power and if I resent they will shoot me and they may as it is. I asked the Lieut. what he meant by this kind of treatment. He said he meant to find out where I had been stopping and who I had been with since I left Camp Ford. He knew, he said, that no Yankee would think of coming into that part of the country unless he had something to come for and someone to come with him, that he knew the country and knew there were some prisoners at Camp Ford who lived in Texas, and he was certain one or more of them had come with me, and he would give me but a little time to tell who I was with and where I had been, and if I did not tell him he would have me out of existence as soon as possible. I did not know what to do or say. I did not want to tell I had been stopping at Brown's house or that I had seen Wallace's father for if I did it was sure death to either family and perhaps myself.

Green began to get impatient. He began to use some not very flattering remarks upon me. I again told him I was alone and had been ever since I left Camp Ford and had stopped at no house overnight. I told him I was acquainted with Wallace who was a prisoner in Camp Ford and who lived in Texas, but I did not leave the Camp with him and did not know as he had any intention of leaving. He told me where his father lived but I could not find him and that I was trying to make my way through to Fort Smith when I called into your father's house for something to eat and you put me under arrest.[4]

He said the scouts had long suspected Wallace and had watched his house; as you see we were obliged to tell a story sometimes and my story did not seem to do much good or to make any impression on him, for he asked me after I had come talking, if that was all I had to say, and if it is I will give you but two minutes to say what you have to say to your maker, so make as much of the time as possible. One Yank out of the way will not be missed. I begged of him to spare my

4 Fort Smith, Arkansas, was under Federal control after 1863. Jeannie M. Whayne, Thomas A. DeBlack, George Sabo, and Morris S Arnold, *Arkansas: A Narrative History* (Fayetteville: University of Arkansas Press, 2013), 212–24.

life and send me back to prison. The answer I got was that my time was about out and he wanted to go back to Camp.

All was silent for about a minute. I would not tell of Wallace or Brown until the last moment for I knew the result would be that the families of both would be put to death. Then I thought of myself, of my dear home, and of the friends I once loved. I thought which was dearer – life and friends, or to expose those who had treated me cruelly and left me alone in this wilderness and friendless country. These thoughts ran through my mind in a few moments, and I thought if I was not shot there might be some possible chance of making my escape and seeing home and friends once more. The guards were ordered to move a few paces back and make ready. This is your last chance said the Lieut; you can either tell me whom you have been with and where you have been or in a minute you will be out of this world. So I proceeded being careful not to speak of Brown's where they all were. I told him I would tell him all if he would spare my life and send me back to Camp Ford. He says, I will spare your life, but I cannot send you back to Camp Ford, so proceed and tell me the truth. I found this was my only chance so I proceeded telling him.

About three weeks ago I left Camp Ford along with a Kansas man and a federal soldier whose name was Wallace and lived in Dallas County. We were to go to Wallace's house and get rations to travel north to the federal lines where we were within fifty miles of his house; they left me in a log cabin asleep. How long they had been gone I did not know, so I inquired and found Wallace's house, his father denied having seen them. But when I told him who I was, and I knew they had been there, he wanted me to promise him that I would not tell of him if I was captured. I stayed there about a week, and heard nothing of my companions when I left. I did not stop at any house only to get something to eat and slept in the woods at night, and this morning I happened in at your father's for something to eat, when you put me under arrest.

So this, Lieut., this is the truth and nothing but the truth and now all I ask is justice. The Lieut. seemed to be very well satisfied with my statement and I was very thankful he was, for not only saving my own life; it had, perhaps, saved the life of Brown's family. They then started me back to camp and I lay down between the guards waiting for morning's dawn. As soon as it was daylight, they ate their breakfast and gave me a small piece of corn bread which was harder than my experience the night before. But I got through with it and felt much better when they were ready to start. The Lieut. left the squad in charge of a Sargent, telling him to report and give Yank up to Col. Bowland[5] and have him dispose of me as he saw fit. Green said he had business to attend to in Dallas and he should not be with them again for several days and then rode off.

---

5 James G. Bourland was colonel of a regiment of Texas cavalry that patrolled the border to ward off Indian raiders and to catch Confederate deserters escaping into Indian Territory (modern-day Oklahoma.) In 1862, as provost marshal, he had overseen the extrajudicial hangings of 41 suspected Unionist residents of the area. Allardice, *Confederate Colonels*, 68; Serge Noirsain, *Les guerres indiennes du Texas et du Nouveau-Mexique: 1825–1875* (Paris: Economica, 2011), 79–87; Richard B. McCaslin, *Tainted Breeze: The Great Hanging at Gainesville, Texas, 1862* (Baton Rouge: Louisiana State University Press, 1994).

12

IMPRISONED IN GAINESVILLE, TEXAS

(SOMETIME IN EARLY 1865)

WE TRAVELED all day and stopped in a deserted log cabin at night. I had not slept any the night before and being very tired and almost worn out by traveling I soon fell asleep. I woke a great many times in the night screaming in my sleep and having frightful dreams. This made me feel weaker and I was afraid I should not be able to travel the next day but morning came and after a scanty meal, I felt stronger. Twice during the day the guards let me ride on of their horses but kept a close look out for me. The third day brought us into Gainesville, Cook County, where Col. Bowland had his headquarters.[1]

It was about four o'clock in the afternoon when we reached there. They rode up to a log cabin and, as we approached it, an old man with grey hair and beard made his appearance along with some confederate officers outside the door. As we came near to them, the old man, who was Col. Bowland, asked who have you there. The answer was, a

---

1 Gainesville is the seat of Cooke County, TX. It is about 60 miles north-northwest of Dallas, and six miles south of the Red River separating Texas from Oklahoma (then called Indian Territory). There was no Confederate army camp in Gainesville, but Bourland's Cavalry made its headquarters there from Jan. 1864 until the end of the war. Wooster, *Lone Star Regiments in Gray*, 219.

James G. Bourland

McCaslin, Tainted Breeze

Yankee. The Colonel looked at me from head to foot and says, well, Yank, you look as if you had had nothing to eat for six months. I reckon you are hungry, ain't you. I said I was both hungry and tired and wanted something to eat and wanted a little rest. He said he was sorry I was hungry for he feared I should have to go to bed without any supper. They kept me here talking and slandering Yankees and calling the Yanks anything but soldiers and loyal men. I had to hear all this but could say nothing. But my thoughts were that some of these fellows would repent for their sayings someday.

The Col. told them to put me in the jail (which was about a quarter of a mile from the quarters on the green) and put two guards over me.[2] When I got to my quarters, the outside looked very comfortable. It was about six feet high and eight feet square. They opened a little door on the side and told me to get in there. I looked in. It was dark, and I could not see

---

2 Maps of Gainesville in 1864 do not survive. If we presume that Bourland's headquarters was in the courthouse, an 1885 map puts the jail one block south of the courthouse. Sanborn Fire Insurance Map, Gainesville, TX, 1885, accessed via Fire Insurance Maps Online.

from one end to the other. Step on that ladder and go ahead, said one of the guards, and, at the same time, giving me a push which sent me in head first. I fell about five feet. When I got up the rebs had their heads at the door laughing at such fun. The door was shut and fastened on the outside.

This was solitary confinement, thought I. I began to explore my mansion. It was five feet underground and only a little filthy straw to make a bed of. It was damp and cold and my scanty clothing was not sufficient to keep me from shivering. I sat in one corner thinking of my lot; of that had happened since I left Camp Ford and what might happen on the morrow. I made up my mind to make my escape, for I had rather run my chance in being shot than be starved to death by these fellows who now call themselves honest and loyal men. There was a short ladder which afforded means to get from this hole to the door. So I got up and sat on the upper rung of this, so that I might hear the conversation of the guards.

13

ESCAPE FROM GAINESVILLE

THEY HAD relieved the guard twice and the third relief I overhead their talk. They had a great deal to say about poor Yank and he understood from the Sargent they were going to hang him in the morning. This was consoling for me to think of, although I was very much interested. One says, suppose he should get away. There ain't any hounds about here, and I pity the boys that are on guard if he should get away. This brought new thoughts into my head and I will wait until the next relief and see what my chance is.

I waited and the next relief was put on duty. I heard the Sargent say it was about one o'clock. After the relief was on about an hour (for they changed them every three hours) and everything was quiet, I spoke to the guard. They told me to shut up and not bother them. I called to him again and told him I wanted to go out on the green a minute if he was willing. He spoke to the other guard who was on the other side of the house, and asked him if he thought it was safe to let me out, he said yes. As soon as I heard the word yes, my whole frame seemed to revive and I felt like a new being. The door was opened and the guard told me to come along.

I left my hat and jacket in the cell and had on nothing but my pants, shoes and a part of a shirt, none of which I had changed for a month or more. I crept up the ladder as if I did not have life enough to walk. As soon as I got outside, they asked me if that was all the clothing I had. I said it was not, for I had left my hat and coat inside. I stood there talking a few minutes, and then asked them where I should go, thinking because I had left my hat and jacket in the cell, I would not attempt to run away. They told me I might go out on the green a little ways if I would hurry back.

I went pulling one leg before the other as if I was most dead. Once three lengths away from them, I was determined not to return alive. I had got about six yards away when they said I had gone far enough. They were both leaning on their guns and facing toward me. This was and perhaps would be my only chance of escape, although it might prove fatal. As soon as they told me to stop I began to fuss with my pants keeping my eyes fixed on them to watch every movement that I might make the best of it. They were busy talking to each other when I stooped and, as I stooped, I started and ran toward the woods which was about a quarter of a mile distant. I had not run more than a dozen steps before the guard hallowed to me to stop and at the same time discharging their rifles at me.

I kept on as fast as I could. The two guards following me and shouting to me to stop. I had gained the woods and so far I felt that I was safe. The two guards did not follow me into the woods. I kept on changing my course to the west, and traveling as fast as I could, for I knew as soon as they got back to camp they would send a squad of rebs after me. I ran the rest of that night, and towards daybreak I came into the road. I looked along the road but could see nobody, so I went back a few rods, and lay down behind some brush.

I was too tired and faint to sleep, so I lay there listening to the birds singing, and watching them as a cat would a canary, wishing I could get my hand on one of them, for I had an appetite to eat almost anything. I lay there about two hours thinking of my situation and what a narrow escape I had had that night, when I heard a whistling. I looked out from my hiding place but could see no one. The sound came nearer and nearer. I watched in the direction, from which the sound came, and soon I saw two negroes coming down the road, each with an ax on his shoulder and when they got nearly opposite to where I was, I came out of the brush and spoke to them. They started to run when I came towards them, thinking there were more of us in the brush. I told them to stop, that I was alone and all I wanted was something to eat. Without asking any questions, they both pulled out of their pockets a piece of corn bread and handed it to me. I thanked them, and asked if there were any scouts around here. They said there was none nearer than Gainesville for how dey had got a Yankee down dar, dat they had caught and day were going to exhibit him and den hang him to the flagpole.[1]

I asked them how far they lived from here, and if their master had gone. They said they lived about a half a mile from here, and dat Massa had gon early this morning. I also asked them if their master was good to them, and if he ever said anything about the Yankees. Massa sais he wishes de Yankees were all dead and if he could help put dem out of de way he would, but I don't' see wat Massa wants to say dat for, for day say how good the Yankees are to de colored folks, and out here da are shooting de colored folks all de time, and I thought you were going to shoot us when we see you, for you look one of de fellows dat do shot. No, said I, I never hurt the colored people for they are always good to me, they give me something to eat when I ask for it. I asked them if they knew which was the nearest way for me to travel to get to the federal lines.

This question seemed to stun them. They first looked at me and then at each other, not knowing what to say. At last

1 This appears to be Federhen's attempt to write in "Negro dialect," a commonly used trope in writing of the period. See, for example, W. S. Scarborough, "Negro Dialect in Fiction," *Unitarian Review*, 32, no. 1 (Jul. 1889), 77–83.

one of them stammered out, yo, yo, you ain't a yankee, are you? Yes, I am, said I, and I know that neither of you will report me, but will do all you can to help me. I am the Yankee that your Master has gone down to Gainesville to see exhibited and to see hung to the flag staff. I got away from there last night, and had got as far as this when I heard you coming, and being very hungry was obliged to ask for something to eat. They were both very uneasy and wanted to go for if Massa should come home and find them not at work, he would whip them, and want to know what they had been doing. They told me as near as they could what direction to take, promising they would not tell a living person that they had seen me. So they both emptied their pockets of corn bread, giving me all they had, wishing that I might get through to the Yankees without being caught. I shook hands with both and bade them goodbye.

They went down the road, and I went back into the brush, to have a good square meal. I was very saving of my rations and would not waste a crumb, for I did not expect to get any more until I reached the federal lines, for I was in hopes to fetch up at that place next. Stopping at a house, I thought, was dangerous work, and I would eat sassafras root and bark of trees before I would risk it again. It was not safe for me to travel in the day, for I might be picked up by some of the scouts and then it would be all up with me. So I went back about a mile in the brush and lay down at the foot of a large tree, and soon fell asleep.

When I awoke the sun was about setting and it began to be dark in the forest, and the frogs began their mournful sounds and the owls their hideous crys. All these sounds were and would sound like so many voices warning me of approaching danger.

14

MORE TRAVELS IN TEXAS

I STARTED and traveled all that night, not seeing or hearing from anyone except now and then I would rout up a group of hogs who would set up an awful grunting, not being much pleased by an intruder coming upon them in their sleep.

At daybreak I came to a large prairie which was as level as a table, and from where I stood I could not see a tree or a bush in any direction. I knew it would be dangerous to cross this by day so I went back into the brush and lay so that I could see all over the prairie.

I slept part of the day and at night I started across the prairie. Just before dark I saw a large amount of smoke off as far as I could see, and as soon as it was dark I saw the prairie was on fire. It was as pretty a sight as I ever saw. How far it was from where I stood I could not judge, but I kept on towards it, the grass not being very long, and it might be morning before I reached it. I was traveling in the northeast direction, but I could not tell what part of the country I was in, nor did I care much.

I felt towards man as I should towards a ferocious animal and if I had a weapon of any kind I would not be captured again by either man or hound. Along towards midnight the fire died away and I had to pick my way by the light of the moon and stars. I traveled by the stars for I knew no other way, and I knew from what I had studied at school the direction from one state to another and the stars answered every purpose of a compass.

15

Recaptured by Confederates

I HAD traveled all night and at day break I was still in the open prairie. The forest was about three miles distant. I thought it best to keep on until I reached it. I reached it about the middle of the morning when I struck a small road.

There was no signs of any settlements and the road had not been traveled over for the grass grew in it as green as on the prairie. Thinking it perfectly safe now to travel in the day I kept on, stopping to rest occasionally and to eat from my scanty rations, for they were fast diminishing. Towards evening I came out on a main road. It was getting dark, and feeling tired I went into the woods to take a nap. I could not sleep for the owls kept screaming and flying down towards me, and if I had slept they would most likely have picked my eyes out. I got up, feeling stiff and sore. It had began to cloud up and the wind was blowing from the north, which was very uncomfortable and cold for one in my situation, having on no hat or jacket and the balance of my clothes were about as good as none.

I had traveled about an hour when I came to a turn in the road, and as I turned the road, there stood two wagons with mules harnessed to them, and a camp fire with about a dozen men sitting about it, chatting and having a good time. As soon as I saw this, I stopped, thinking what to do. Perhaps, thought I, it might be some of Col Bowlands' scouts and, if they were to capture me, they would show me no mercy. So I turned to go back.

As I was turning a dog jumped from one of the wagons towards me growling and barking. I turned to see if any of the men were coming to see what the matter was with the dog, and at the same instant one of the men who was up from his seat at the first bark of the dog sung out for me to halt, but instead of halting I started and ran towards the brush. He shouted for me to halt again, answered by the shot of a musket. The ball of which sent a very unpleasant breeze past my head and lodged in a tree in front of me. The dog was close onto my heels and I knew it would be useless for me to try to get away from him, so I stopped and waited until they got up to where I was.

I told them I was unarmed and meant no harm. They escorted me back to the camp fire and then wanted to know who I was, and the reason I was lurking about their wagon. I told them I was a paroled prisoner from Camp Ford on my way home in Ohio and I travelled both night and day for I had a great many hundred miles to travel before I could get transportation, and as I was passing your wagon, a dog jumped from one and I ran to get out of his way.

I asked them to what command they belonged, for I feared they might be some of Col. Bowlands' scouts, and, if they were, I made up my mind not to spend the night with them. They said they were Gen. McCollough's[1] scouts, and they were out on the lookout for deserters, and they were very glad to pick me up for they were just returning without any prisoners. I told them I thought it was very hard of them to take me off my road and thus detain me for I am certain that

---

1 Brig. Gen. Henry Eustace McCulloch was commander of the Northern Subdistrict of the District of Texas, New Mexico, and Arizona, from Aug. 29, 1863, to the end of the war. John E. Eicher and David J. Eicher, *Civil War High Commands* (Stanford, CA: Stanford University Press, 2001), 376.

Gen. McCollough will release me as soon as he knew who I was.

If we had any assurance that you were all right, we would let you pass on. Let me look at your parole papers and pass, and, if they are all right, you may go. I told them that I had been robbed on the road and had had my hat, coat, and bag along with my papers taken from, so I had not proof only my word as a soldier. They believed my story was true and asked me if I was hungry. I said I was that I had not had anything to eat for two days. One of them pulled out a piece of bacon from his saddle bag and another a piece of corn bread and warmed them before the fire and I sat down and had what seemed to me to be the best meal I had ever eaten.

After I had eaten my supper they wanted me to stop overnight with them, for they said they were afraid I would lose my way as it was so dark. I accepted this invitation for I was only too glad to get shelter for the night. We sat around the fire until it was quite late smoking and talking about the war. They spread some blankets on the grass and I slept sound all night. In the morning they made a fire and cooked breakfast. One of them gave me an old hat and jacket to wear. When I told them, with their liberty, I would go on with my journey, and that I felt very grateful towards them for their kind treatment to me.

As I was about to start one of them says to me suppose you wait a few minutes—we are going your way and I think we shall want you to accompany us. I asked him what he meant, for you are traveling east and I am to travel north. It makes no difference which way you are travelling, says the reb. If I had thought you all right last night I should have let you go, but, as it is, I shall be under the obligation of putting you under guard until we reach Barnum which is Gen. McCollough's headquarters and, if you attempt to get away, it will go hard

Henry E. McCulloch

McCaslin, Tainted Breeze

with you, and, if you are all right, when you have seen the General, he will let you go and give you rations.[2]

I asked him how long it would take us to get there, hoping we might have another night to sleep in the woods so as to give me another chance to make my escape. He said we would arrive there about four o'clock that afternoon. I felt rather blue about this time and wished I was safe back inside of Camp Ford stockade. They soon harnessed their mules into the wagons and were ready to start. The men were all mounted so they put me in a wagon for safe keeping.

It had begun to rain, and by the time we reached Barnum which was about five o'clock in the evening it was raining quite hard and the Gen. and the other officers had gone home. So they locked me up in a small empty room, there to stay until morning. I slept on the floor and in the morning about ten o'clock I was called out and brought before the

2 Bonham, TX, was the headquarters of McCulloch's command; it is about 55 miles east of Gainesville. David Paul Smith, *Frontier Defense in the Civil War: Texas' Rangers and Rebels* (College Station: Texas A&M University Press, 1992), 72.

General and several other officers. The General received me very kindly and wanted to know all the particulars about Camp Ford and about my parole papers. He said that he was very sorry that I had been robbed of my parole papers for it would put me to a great deal of trouble and inconvenience. He said he did not doubt my story, but he should be obliged to keep me under guard until he could hear from Camp Ford. His adjutant was an ugly looking fellow. He told the General he bet I was a runaway from the prison, or else a spy from General Blunt's army, and that I better be looked.[3]

The General did not have much to say after this speech, but told the adjutant to see that I was put under guard until he could hear from Camp Ford. He took my name, the State and Battery to which I belonged and said he would see to it as soon as possible.

3 Brig. Gen. James Gilpatrick Blunt commanded Union troops in the District of the Frontier, which encompassed the southern tier of Missouri counties, Kansas, and the Indian Territory, from Jun. 9, 1863, to Apr. 17, 1864. From Oct. 10, 1864, to the end of the war he commanded the District of South Kansas and the First Division of the Army of the Border under Gen. Samuel Curtis. After Jan. 1865, Blunt held command over the Indian Territory. Robert Collins, *General James G. Blunt: Tarnished Glory* (Gretna, LA: Pelican Publishing Co., 2005), 130, 186–89, 210.

16

IMPRISONED IN BONHAM, TEXAS

THE ADJUTANT along with two guards escorted me to a log cabin about a mile from the General's headquarters. It was a small shanty but was much more comfortable than the one I had left in Gainesville.

When I entered my new home I was surprised to find it occupied by a young man about my own age, and had a fearless look in his eye. As the adjutant closed the door, he said to my companion, here Bill, here is a Yank for you to play with. This was introduction enough, for as soon as the door was closed we were acquainted with each other. I told him how I had got there and about my being robbed. He said he reckoned he knew the parties who had done it, for he had just been captured away from his company while he was stealing chickens, and if his company knew where he was they would battle the town but what they would have him released.

I asked him his name and to what company he belonged. He said his name was Bill Grandstaff[1] and he belonged to

---

1 There are a number of men named William Grandstaff who appear in the records of the Confederate armies, but none are listed as part of Quantrill's troops. Quantrill's men were irregulars and the composition of his command changed often, so they were not always recorded. The 1910 census shows a William Grandstaff, born in 1846, who lived in the part of Missouri where Quantrill recruited his men.

Quantrell's band of scouts.[2] We talked that night until it was quite late and the guard told us we had better hold our tongues and go to sleep. There were three guards over us. One at the rear of the cabin and the other two in front. There was a thick forest about an eighth of a mile from the rear of the cabin, called the Bardark River swamps.[3]

When Bill was captured, he had his horse taken from him, besides his revolvers and his knife and all they left him was his blankets which we had to sleep on.

2 In late 1861, William Clarke Quantrill organized a band of guerillas that grew from ten men to around 400. After Aug. 15, 1862, his unit was considered part of the regular Confederate Army under the terms of the Partisan Ranger Act. During 1862 and 1863, Quantrill's Raiders engaged in guerilla warfare throughout Missouri and Kansas. Following a raid on Lawrence, Kansas, in Aug. 1863 during which they reportedly killed more than 150 civilians, Quantrill's Raiders retreated to a camp on Mineral Creek, about 15 miles northwest of Sherman, TX, and wintered there. This camp was about 40 miles from Bonham. Due to the havoc that Quantrill's men inflicted on the citizens of Sherman, Henry McCulloch ordered them to report for duty in the vicinity of Corpus Christi. Quantrill refused the order, and on Mar. 30, 1864, McCulloch had him arrested in Bonham. Quantrill quickly escaped. Internal strife split Quantrill's Raiders into two groups, one commanded by Bill Anderson and the other by George Todd. They raided in Missouri in 1864 and were defeated in several engagements with Union troops. Quantrill's men never returned to Texas, and Quantrill himself rode east through Tennessee and into Kentucky, where he was killed by Union troops in May 1865. If Grandstaff had been taken prisoner during the winter of 1863–64, it would likely have been for criminal activity rather than during a battle. Edward E. Leslie, *The Devil Knows How to Ride: The True Story of William Clarke Quantrill and His Confederate Raiders* (New York: Random House, 1996); Duane Schultz, *Quantrill's War: The Life and Times of William Clarke Quantrill, 1837–1865* (New York: St. Martin's Press, 1996).

3 Bois d'Arc Creek runs north-northeast about a mile east of Bonham. It drains into the Red River about 25 miles northeast of the city.

17

ESCAPE FROM BONHAM

THE NEXT morning we were called to get our rations, which consisted of a pint of coarse wheat and a piece of bacon for each of us. There was a little fireplace in one end of the cabin where we had to cook our own food, and the third guard answered as an errand boy, for he would bring us wood and water.

The next night after we had laid down, Billy asked me what I thought about getting away from here. He said perhaps it might prove fatal to both of us, and we might get away without a scratch. I told him I was ready at any time, for I had got tired of this kind of life, and did not care much whether I killed them or whether they killed me, but I have made up my mind to do one or have done with the other. So he said we must both be ready at any minute. We stayed there about ten days.

This day was Sunday, so they said, for I did not know one day from another. It was raining quite hard and had been all day, and about the middle of the afternoon, as we were sitting by the fireplace planning our escape, an old man entered the cabin with a book in his hand, saying he had come to read to us from the Bible and to have a talk with us. The guards stood around the door to hear what the old man had to say. He read and explained a chapter but Bill and myself could not have told what he had said five minutes after, for our minds were too much occupied in making our escape that night. We thanked the old man and he went off singing "America"; it was growing dark and one of the guards had gone off to his supper.[1] After we had finished our supper, I was standing in the doorway talking with one of the guards and not being prepared or thinking at that moment about breaking away and not noticing Bill's movements, when in an instant Bill struck the guard across the face with a piece of heavy wood which he had taken from the fireplace falling him to the ground and, as his rifle dropped, it went off. Bill gave me a push and we both started round the cabin for the brush. The guard in the rear hearing the report of a musket came to his comrade's relief, and, as we ran on one side, the guard came round on the other, so before he could see what the trouble was, we had got the start of them. We had not got many rods before three musket shots were fired after us. We kept on and soon we reached the brush. Here we changed our course, and went east towards the Red River.[2]

We travelled all that night and lay in the brush the next day. I asked him where he intended to go and if he had any idea of going through to the federal lines. He said he was going to where his company was and he wanted me to go with him, and, after we had got there, everything would be all right. Before I enlisted in the Army, I had read and seen a great many horrible pictures in the illustrated newspapers which had been committed by Quantrall's and other guerilla bands and I was rather timid about going any further with

1 This is probably the song also known as "My Country 'Tis of Thee," written by Samuel Francis Smith in 1832. By the time of the Civil War, it was commonly used in hymnals and sung in Independence Day celebrations. Ace Collins, *Songs Sung Red, White, and Blue: The Stories Behind America's Best-Loved Patriotic Songs* (New York: HarperResource, 2003): 128–35.

2 Presumably they took a northeasterly route. They would have eventually encountered the Red River by traveling directly east from Bonham, but it is almost 100 miles away in that direction.

A settler's hut on the Red River in Texas

Library of Congress

him, for my being a Yankee, they might accidentally give me a shot.

Night came and we started towards the river.[3] We traveled that night and the next until about midnight. When we came to a small river, we got two logs and tied them together with strips of bark so as to make a boat.[4] We paddled our boat down the river and towards morning, we came to a small plantation and the house was close to the river. We pulled towards shore and went up to the house.

As we approached, a young negro man came to the door half dressed and looked as if he was just out of bed, and wanted to know what we wanted. Neither of us answered him

3 Federhen likely means the Red River.

4 Depending on the distance and direction traveled during the night, this may have been Bergher Creek or Pine Creek.

until we got up close to the cabin, and just as we were about to speak to tell him what we wanted, he shut the door in our face. Both of us were hungry, not having anything to eat but a few wild onions since we left Barnum. This made us rather vexed, so we tried the door and found the Negro had locked it. Bill hallowed to him and told him he wanted something to eat, and, if he did not open the door, he would break it in. We listened for an answer, but we heard nothing. In another minute, we broke the door open and went in.

We looked around for the nigger but he was not to be found. I looked out of a window in the rear of the cabin and saw the nigger running across the field as if someone was after him. Bill said that it would not do to stay here long, for the Negro would go and report us, so look around and see what we can find. We upset everything in the cabin and found some corn cakes and some dried beef, also some clothing and a pair of Yankee blankets all of which we were in want of very much. We took what we wanted and left in a hurry for the river where we left our boat.

When we got there, we found it gone. It had drifted down the river out of sight. Bill said it was no use going down the river any further, for we were only going out of our way, while we can cross the river here and travel through the woods and get to his company's camp quicker than if we paddled down to Red River. So we made a small raft and crossed the river, taking care to destroy the raft so as to leave no trace for our pursuers in case we had any.

We traveled all day and night and the next day until about noon. When we came to the Red River, there was a plantation on the other side and Bill said that he knew where he was now, for he had been to the house to buy meal and butter milk and the camp was about ten miles northeast of it.[5]

I told Bill as soon as we reached the river that I was going to leave him and run my chances in getting down to where the federal fleet was.[6] He said he thought there was no site for me to get through so I had better come with him and live and lead an easy life. He said that I should have a good horse to ride and enough of good clothing to wear. I thought it policy[7] to go with him, so we started up the river bank, not seeing or hearing from anyone.

---

5 It is impossible to reconcile the timing of Federhen's account with the historical record. All of Quantrill's troops had ridden to Missouri by the beginning of May 1864, a time when Federhen was still in Louisiana. However, some of Federhen's recollections regarding Quantrill that follow can be verified as having taken place in the spring of 1864. It may be that Federhen fell in with another band of brigands who presented themselves as members of Quantrill's Raiders, and that one of them even impersonated "Bloody Bill" Anderson. Albert Castel and Thomas Goodrich, *Bloody Bill Anderson: The Short, Savage Life of a Civil War Guerilla* (Mechanicsburg, PA: Stackpole Books, 1998), 37.

6 Although it is difficult to figure how Federhen would have learned it, after May 21, 1864, Confederate troops controlled the length of the Red River down to Simmesport, LA (which is on the Atchafalaya River just south of the point where it branches from the Red River). Widespread desertions in the spring of 1865, followed by the formal surrender of the Trans-Mississippi Theater on May 26, left the river open to Federal boats. Thomas W. Cutrer, *Theater of a Separate War: The Civil War West of the Mississippi River, 1861–1865* (Chapel Hill: University of North Carolina Press, 2017), 404, 434–37.

7 In nineteenth century usage, the word "policy" without a modifier signified "prudent conduct; politic or expedient behaviour; prudence, shrewdness, sagacity." *Oxford English Dictionary.*

18

IN QUANTRILL'S CAMP

WE TRAVELED the rest of that day and that night until about ten o'clock when we came in sight of camp fires. He was not sure this was his camp and perhaps it would be dangerous for us to approach it any nearer until morning. So we spread our blankets and layed down. We were both soon asleep and slept until daylight.

The next morning the sun had been shining bright for about an hour before we awoke and everything looked cheerful and pleasant. We got up, shook and folded our blankets and set about making a raft to cross the river for the camp was a quarter of a mile from the other bank. We crossed the river and started towards the camp.[1]

As we came nearer, Bill recognized some of the boys and shouted to them. They knew him and there was a general shouting and cheering through the camp. Here comes Bill Grandstaff, but the time we reached them, the whole camp

---

1 In early Apr. 1864, Quantrill and his men briefly made camp in Choctaw country, which extended along the north bank of the Red River from the 96th meridian to the Arkansas boundary and was thus just a few miles northeast of Bonham. Leslie, *The Devil Knows How to Ride*, 299; Roy Gittinger, *The Formation of the State of Oklahoma* (Norman: University of Oklahoma Press, 1939), map 4.

William Clarke Quantrill

Leslie, *The Devil Knows How to Ride*

was ready to shake hands with him and I thought they would shake him in pieces.

I was quite forgotten when some of the boys asked Bill who that chap was he had along with him. He told them that I had been a Yankee prisoner, and was put in the same cell with him and by my means he had made his escape from old Gen. McCollough's clutches and, if it had not been for Yank, I do not know if you would ever have seen me again. So, boys, use him well and call him one of us.

Quantrall had taken a company of his men and gone into eastern Arkansas to make a raise, as they called it,[2] and had left a small company of fifty men under the command of Capt. Bill Anderson[3] to look after their own interests.

After I had been welcomed into their camp, we had a good breakfast provided for us which consisted of boiled chicken and wheat biscuit and a cup of coffee. We both ate with a good relish, and, after we had done, the boys furnished us with

2 There is a brief record of a raid by Quantrill on Fort Smith, Arkansas, in Apr. 1864. Leslie, *The Devil Knows How to Ride*, 299.

3 Anderson and Quantrill parted while Quantrill was still in Texas.

pipes and tobacco. Bill or I did not do anything that day but rest ourselves and lay about smoking and telling the boys about our escape. Towards evening, as I was passing Capt. Anderson's tent, he called me in. He is about five feet, six inches in height, and was dressed in a full Capt.'s uniform, with two revolvers in his belt, which he said he never intended to be without. I sat down by the side of the bank and we soon entered into conversation.

He wanted to know where I was from and what branch of the service I belonged to. I told him I was from Boston and I was in the Artillery service. He asked me a great many questions about the North, for he said he was as good a Union man at the breaking out of the war as ever any man could be, but the federals drove him away from home in Missouri. I asked how that was.

19

BILL ANDERSON'S STORY

HE SAID in the year of 1862, I was living in Missouri with my father, mother and sister, a girl of eighteen years, not wishing to enter the army, and my parents being old they need my services on the farm.[1] Along about the first of the year there were several independent companies of federal soldiers about the state and in other bordering states which the people feared, for they had destroyed and killed many families. One morning in the month of July, as I was at work in the front garden, I heard horses and heard men shouting and not a great way off. The house sat in back from the road and was surrounded by thick woods. I hurried out and looked up the road from behind the trees to see what was coming, when I was much

[1] The story told by Federhen is not found in any biography of Anderson. In fact, Anderson's mother died in 1860 after being struck by lightning, and his father was killed in 1861 during a dispute over horse rustling. Anderson lost a sister when a building being used as a federal prison in Kansas City, MO, collapsed in 1863. Anderson began his paramilitary career as Jayhawker—a brigand who preyed upon Kansans with Confederate sympathies. When he spotted better opportunities he switched to bushwhacking, which was the same activity with Unionist victims. Anderson fell in with Quantrill's band in 1863. He was known as "Bloody Bill" because he used violence against military enemies and civilians alike. Castel and Goodrich, *Bloody Bill Anderson*, 12–19; Leslie, *The Devil Knows How to Ride*, 103. As noted in Chapter 17, other brigands may have presented themselves as Anderson and his cohort.

William
"Bloody Bill" Anderson

Castel and Goodrich,
Bloody Bill Anderson

surprised to see about twenty federal soldiers all dressed in blue, well mounted. They were close to the house and the thought struck me that they were going to destroy my home.

I started into the brush for I knew there would not be time for me to get to the house before they could shoot me. I lay down under some brush which I had piled up to burn. Here I lay, my heart burning with fear. I had not layed more than two minutes before the horsemen showed themselves and in an instant they surrounded the house and fired a volley into the house. I knew if I showed myself, it would be sure death, so I lay still, my heart burning with rage.

In a few moments my father and old man opened the door to inquire what was the matter, and as soon as he showed himself he was shot dead and fell on the ground in front of his old home. The soldier shouted out for the rest of them to come out, they kept firing into the house at last one of the soldiers sung out there goes the old woman she has gone up, I knew that this was my mother she was shot in the house, where was my sister they had stopped there firing and some of them entered the house soon, soon I heard the shrieks of my sister, she too was a victim, I could hear about every word they spoke and I knew by their actions and their talk that they were brutally killing her, my brain was almost turned and only hopes of avenging their deaths kept me quiet for my blood was boiling with revenge.

I did not know any of these men but from where I lay I could look through the brush and mark each man's countenance so that I would know anyone of them in case I should ever meet with them after they had murdered my father mother and sister. They drug them to the rear of the house and threw them into a well and then set fire to the house and left. They then went along the road burning houses and murdering the people. I lay there until they had gone and then went to try to save some things but the fire had destroyed everything. I looked down the well to give the last look at my dear parents and sister.

I was almost crazy. One hour, before, my home was a happy one, but now all was dead and my home destroyed, what was I to do, my only recourse now was to join a guerilla company and to be revenge, for this had drove me desperate and I swore I would not leave a Yankee settlement in Missouri that I would kill and burn down every house that sheltered a federal soldiers, who could blame me for it. I left the once happy home to find relief amongst strangers, I had heard of Quantrill and knew he was in Arkansas,[2] and I was determined to find him and to join his company for I knew some of the boys in the company, so I traveled along for about two weeks when I found them, my old companions were glad to see me, and after I had told them what had happened, they welcomed me into their company, they furnished me with revolvers and a horse, and after I had been with them a few days Quantrill told me that he thought of making a raid in Missouri and if I wanted to I could take 50 men and start, and that he would go with the rest of his men into the eastern part

---

2 Quantrill's men spent Nov. 1862 through May 1863 in Arkansas. Schultz, *Quantrill's War*, 127–30.

of Kansas for some of his boys had some Yanks there that they wanted to raid upon.

I took 50 of the best men and started, we did not take any rations with us, we calculated on feeding on the country, each man was armed with two revolvers and a knife, and some had rifles, this was new business for me, but I had got desperate, and I cared little for life and was bound to destroy everything and every man that wore the Yankee blue, we went into Missouri and had several slight skirmishes with federal companies, but never amounted to much.[3]

Once I captured 10 federal soldiers, a lieutenant and nine men. We took everything away from them, tied them to a tree, and then shot them. They plead and beg for mercy, but the thoughts of my parents and sister being killed by federal soldiers I would not have spared one of them if they had been my dearest friends for I was death on anything that had on blue.

3 Anderson is recorded as leading a band of 30 to 40 men in Lafayette and Johnson counties, Missouri, in the summer of 1863. Castel and Goodrich, *Bloody Bill Anderson*, 23–24.

20

FIRST RAID WITH QUANTRILL'S MEN

IT WAS getting quite late and the horn had been blown for supper, so I left the captain's tent and went to my quarters. The boys were at supper and had quite forgotten yank, they made room and shared with me. After supper we lighted our pipes and set up quite late talking about the war.

They asked me all sorts of questions about the north, they seem to be ignorant of what a city was, they wanted to know if Boston had many houses, and how so many folks got a living, and wanted to know if they were not all farmers and herds men. I explained it to them, told them how many inhabitants there are and how many different trades there were carried on, and about the schools churches and institutions. They were very much interested and wanted to know if I knew how to write, and if I did they wished I would learn them. I told him I would and I would give them the first lesson in the morning, some of the boys did know but the most of them were brought up on a farm, and did not know how to read spell or write.

It was very late and we all retired to our tent. Billy and I occupied one tent and had a good strong mattress to lay on. The tent that covered us was marked U.S. and also the blankets that we had to cover us so it seemed by my being well treated, and sleeping under the US letters that I must be inside the federal lines. We slept well that night, and the next day some of the boys were going out to steal chickens, and asked Bill and myself to go with them, and we went each of us had a horse to ride and a revolver.

We rode about 15 miles that morning stopping at almost every house to get something to eat or drink, the strangest thing we could get to drink was buttermilk, and the boys said I would get fat drinking it if I stayed with them six weeks, and I think I was sorely in need of something for I was as poor as a crow.[1]

We rode up to an old man's house, and asked him if he had any chickens to sell. He said no that he only had a few chickens, and then he did not want to lose, and while we were talking with the old man two of the boys went to the rear of the house and robbed the hencoop of about a dozen chickens, and had a rope around a pig leg pulling him along after them, as they came round to where the rest of us were, one of them sung out, come boys the old fellow hasn't any chickens to sell so we might as well go along. As we turned our horses to go the old man asked us if we were not going to pay him for his chickens and pigs that we were carrying off. One of the boys answered and said, you told us you did not have any chickens to sell, so we took what we could find.

We went back towards camp stopping at houses along the road, to get corn and fodder. When we stopped at a house some of the boys would dismount, and ask if they had any corn for sale, and after setting the price they were to pay for it, they would put it into their sacks, tie it on behind their saddles, and without paying for it, they would thank them and bid them good morning and ride off. When we got back to camp the boys asked me how I liked the fun, I told them that it was such fun that I had not been used to having, but I suppose I should get used to it after a few days.

---

1 This idiom is thought to originate in the observation that crows, who winter in the north, are seen eating sand and gravel to fill their stomachs when food is scarce before springtime. "The Crow," *Connecticut School Journal* 7, no. 26 (1902), 7.

We ate our supplies and then sat around the campfires telling all sorts of stories. It was quite late when we went to bed so they let us sleep until the sun had been shining about three hours.

21

A Story of a
Foraging Party in Missouri

THERE WAS not much going on in camp for several days, and we amused ourselves playing cards. One afternoon a company of 25 men started on a forager's expedition into Missouri. They traveled that night and the next two days until about 11 o'clock that night[1] when they saw a campfire some distance ahead they halted, tied their horses and then started towards the campfire keeping a smart look out for the pickets.[2]

As they came near the camp they separated and soon three of the boys came into the picket. The guard summoned them to halt asking them who they were. The boys told him they were all right, that they were going back to camp, and the guard supposing they were some of his own men. They came nearer to him and he not being on his guard they seized him and told him if he made any noise, that they would cut

1 While Federhen's account is not precise, one can infer that the location of the camp was near the north bank of the Red River. From any point along the Red River it is around 250 miles to the nearest part of Missouri. Even the fastest horses cannot travel this distance in two days.

2 The pickets were soldiers assigned to keep watch at a distance from the main body of soldiers, often a quarter mile from the edge of camp. Wright, *The Language of the Civil War*, 229–30.

him in pieces. The boys made him tell how many there was in camp, and to what command they belonged. After they had found out all they wanted, they took the guard and tied him to a tree, gagged him and left him there.

The camp was quiet, there only being one picket out, so they surrounded the camp and from a single shot they all rushed into the camp yelling and shouting and making it sound as if there were 100 men or more. The whole camp was aroused but not a gun was fired, this sudden attack did not give them time to think of their arms so they were obliged to surrender. Some of them were not half dressed, others were half asleep, wanting to know what was the matter. They said that they had not done anything, and they did not see what such a rumpus was kicked up about. The sergeant who was in command of the boys, ordered them to search the prisoners, and take away all firearms and knives. The boys went to work and not only taking their arms, they cleaned out their pockets of almost everything.

After this was done they were drawn up into line and marched off, they released the guard they had tied to the tree and then got their horses. They march them two days without anything to eat, and when about five miles from where the rest of us were, they halted at an old mill, and close to the mill was a stockade which had been used for a cattle pen. The stockade was about eight feet high, and the post pointed so that it was impossible for anyone to climb over the top.

There was a stream of water that ran close by one end of the stockade which had been used to supply the milk. The boys let the prisoners get what water they wanted to drink and then told them that they expected to meet a company here, that we're going to take them to Shreveport and while they were waiting they must all go inside of the stockade for safekeeping. The prisoners believing the story true, all went into the pen.

The pen was small but they had just room enough to stir about without crowding one another. After they were all in the gate was fastened on the outside. After this was done the boys, (or brutes you might call them) encircled the pen and began shooting in among the prisoners. The boys kept up their firing until every prisoner fell. You can imagine the feelings of these poor fellows when they found and saw death staring them in the face, they could not get out of their confinement, and if they did it would only be sure death to them. A few they found out their situation. Some of them cried others were praying and calling on God to protect their wives and families but their cries soon died out for every man was shot.

After they had finished this villainous crime they opened the gate and what men were not dead, they soon finished with their revolvers. The boys then went into the pen, and ruffled the dead men's pockets taking their watches and what other jewelry they wore, and cutting off their fingers, to get the rings which they wore and putting them on their own fingers. In an hour after this the boys came back in camp cheering and rejoicing over their fun and their plunder. Most of them had two watches besides rings jewelry and a great many other articles such as photographs and letters which had been sent from the homes of the unfortunate.

There was some excitement in the camp after the boys had got home for a squad of boys had gone off and had some whiskey and they were full of fight. They wanted to share with the others of their plunder, but they were quieted by the captain who made his appearance and told them if they did not make less noise about it, he would stop some of their breaths.

Then most of them went to make their tents and everything went off quiet the rest of the day.

22

A Second Raid
with Quantrill's Men

IN THE morning after we had got our breakfast Billy and some of the other boys proposed going off on a scout and wanted yank to go with them so we saddled our horses and armed ourselves with two revolvers each and a knife and started, there were eight of us.

We went towards the southern part of Arkansas stopping at a house to get our dinners and not paying for them, we got some chickens at another house and roasted them for supper and slept in the barn that night. The next morning we started off early.

About noon as we were passing a large farmhouse we see some chickens in the front yard two of the boys dismounted and jumped over the fence to catch them. They made some noise in trying to catch them, and the noise brought two darkies out of a little cabin to see what the matter was. They both came screaming to save the chickens, the foremost darky sung out to the boys to leave the chicks alone, and if you don't I will call Massa. He had no more than got the words out of his mouth before a shot from one of the boys revolver brought him to the ground and the other darkie ran away. The boys caught up a half a dozen chicks and got on their horses and we rode until late in the afternoon when we halted at a large farmhouse. As we halted a man about 40 years of age showed himself at the door. The sergeant who was with us asked him if he could furnish quarters for his men and horses. The farmer said he could and asked us into the house, we tied our horses to the fence and went in. The farmer was very polite and wanted to know if we had had anything to eat. The sergeant said no and that his men and horses were both hungry. One of the boys went out and brought in the chickens they had stole for the farmer and his wife to cook. They cut them in pieces and made a good chicken stew, after supper we put our horses into the barn and gave them plenty of corn and fodder. We went back into the house and sat up talking until it was quite late and then the farmer showed us to our room. The eight of us slept in one room on some straw and we had our blankets to cover us, so we slept sound all night.

In the morning we were called and had our breakfast of cornbread and fried bacon. When we were ready to go the farmer helped us to get our horses, and while we were in the barn the farmer said that he had some very nice tobacco in the house if we wanted to bring any. The boys said that they did, so they went back to the house to settle our bill for supper breakfast and lodging, and to get some tobacco. The sergeant asked how much his bill was for his men and horses, the farmer thought a few moments and then said give me $15 a head right through or five dollars a head and silver.[1] The sergeant told him that he thought that was too big a price to ask, and asked him if that was the best he could do. He said it was for he had to pay heavy taxes and corn and food was scarce and very high, the sergeant and boys did not feel

---

1 The farmer was negotiating a higher amount in paper currency than in coin because inflationary pressures had pushed the value of Confederate paper currency to a fraction of the value of coins of the same denomination. For example, in Mar. 1863, a gold dollar was worth $3.25 in paper. By the same time in 1864, the gold dollar bought 26 paper dollars, and in 1865, $70. James F. Morgan, *Graybacks and Gold: Confederate Monetary Policy* (Pensacola, FL: Perdido Bay Press, 1985), 120–21.

satisfied with these high prices for provisions, and told the farmer that they would only give him two dollars in silver for each man and horse. The farmer was angry at this and called the sergeant a thief, and said that he would be hanged before he would take less than five dollars in silver for each man and horse.

The boys would not have troubled the farmer if he had set a fair price for his food, but as it was they paid him his five dollars in silver and then asked him to show his tobacco. The farmer went to a closet and pulled out a bushel basket full of twisted tobacco.[2] The sergeant asked what he asked a pound. Three dollars in silver was the ready reply. Thinking he had made well on his prisoners he was going to double on his tobacco, and seeing the boys had plenty of money he thought of making his fortune.

The boys were helping themselves and filling their pockets. The farmer thinking he would not get paid for all told us to take it out of their pockets and he would count the twist, before they weighed a pound each. We did not pay any attention to what he said but kept on, leaving but a few twists in the basket. He asked if we did not intend to pay for it. One of the boys answering said I reckon not.

I seen the farmer was getting quite angry and as I was standing nearest to him and wishing to be a little safer distance I turned to go and as soon as I turned my back he grabbed me by the throat and said if I did not put that tobacco back that he would choke me. We scuffled a few minutes while he was trying to get one hand into my pocket and the other around my throat. My revolvers were in my belt behind and my bowie knife was in my breast. I tried to get my pistols

---

2 Tobacco leaves were twisted together to form a rope of tobacco, from which smaller pieces could be cut; this process of preserving tobacco was utilized at least as far back as the seventeenth century. Jordan Goodman, ed., *Tobacco in History and Culture* (Detroit: Thomson Gale, 2005), 1:127.

but it was no use, I could not let go my hold long enough but what he would get the best of me so I let them go. In our scuffle he had torn my jacket and shirt open, and my throat was feeling rather uncomfortable. I called the boys to take him off, but all the answer I got was go in yank I bet on you.

I seen that my position was a desperate one, so I grappled the harder. I had my forefinger on my left hand in his eye and was trying to gouge it out when he from pain released his grasp from my throat to take my hand off his face, and at the same instant he let go my throat. I drew my knife from my breast and buried it twice into the body of my rebel friend. He let go his hold and I pushed him off. He staggered a few steps back then fell in a fainting fit.

I looked around for my companions they were all standing at one end of the room cheering and hurrahing for yanks victory. I was almost crazy from excitement and to think of what I had done just for a few pounds of tobacco made me still worse. The Farmer's wife was screaming and taking on a fearful rate pulling her hair and clapping her hands and coming towards me as if she would tear me to pieces. I shrank from her for she was almost crazy with rage thinking that I had killed her husband. A little girl about 10 years of age who was the farmer's daughter, was sent by her mother to the nearest neighbor who lived about two miles distant.

I bent over the man to see if he was dead, but he was not. The boys brought some water and bathed his head and washed his wounds so in a short time he recovered. While the boys were bathing him some of them raffled his pockets and took the silver they had paid him for his board besides other things he had in his pockets. Then pulling him into one corner of the room, layed him on some straw, and then we left him at the house along with some chickens which we found running about in the yard. I stopped at the well then washed my hands and knife for they were both covered with blood. We mounted our horses and rode on.

We changed our course and started back towards camp on another road. We rode that day and slept in a barn at night. The next day we stopped at houses and got our meals and a good supply of meal and wheat for the camp without costing anything. Instead of going direct back to camp we took a road north of where the camp was so as to see the place where the yanks were killed a few days before. We searched there the next day and it was just as they had left it. The bodies lay piled on top of the other and it was a heart sick sight to look at. The birds and wild hogs had been feasting from their bodies and their faces were all picked to the bone. We did not stay there long but made our way back to camp.

We reached there about the middle of the afternoon. I for one was glad to get back, for I was tired of riding, and more tired of the life I was leading. I was feeling rather blue, and I did not care much whether I was put out of existence or not. I did not eat any supper and the boys laughed at me, and said I would get used to it after I had been out on another scout.

I did not mind anything more they said but went to my tent and lay down to try and get some sleep, but no sleep for me, my mind was everywhere but in its right place. I would lay a while and then get up light my pipe and try to think of something else, but all I could see and think of, was about the man I had had the scuffle with and could see his wife and daughter bending over his lifeless form. These thoughts were in my mind and I could not drive them out. It was getting late and soon Billy came to turn in. I told him that I did not feel very well. He took his canteen from under his bunk and told me to take a drink of spirits and then I would feel all right. I took a good drink and soon felt more like lying down than standing up.

I fell asleep and in the morning I felt much better after I had washed and eaten my breakfast. I stayed about camp for several days not wishing to go with them on anymore scouts at present.

23

A Third Raid
with Quantrill's Men

ONE DAY some of the boys were going over the river into Texas for there was a sick old rebel who lived there and they wanted to get some of his money and wanted yank to go with them so nine of us saddled our horses and started.

We forded the river and about noon we reached a log cabin around which grew a number of peach trees, it full bloom besides flowers in green vines running over the cabin. It was as pleasant a place as I had seen. As we rode up a little boy came running out and wanted to know, what we wanted. One of the boys asked him if his folks were at home. The little fellow said that his mother had taken the old horse and had gone to the mill to get some corn for us to eat, and father is sick in bed or else he would have gone. One of the boys asked him if he knew the way to the mill, and if he did, that he had better go and find his mother and tell her to come home. The boy said he knew where the mill was and it was about four miles up the road, but he did not want to leave his sick father. They told the boy to take his hat and go after his mother and that they would take good care of his father until he returned.

We dismounted our horses and tied them to the fence, and then we went into the house. They sent the boy off and as soon as he was gone they went into the room where there was an old gray headed man lying on the bed with his eyes half closed and looking more like a corpse then a human being. As we entered the room the old man looked up and saluted us five saying good morning gentlemen. One of the boys took hold of the bed clothes and pulled them down telling him that they had come after his money, and if he did not give it up, or tell them where it was, they would hang him. The old man looked up and said he had no money, and if he had they should have it all rather than they should harm him. He said he had done all he could to help the poor boys in the field, and had given them all he had both in money and food and had no money left.

The old man closed his eyes and shook his head but this did not satisfy the boys for some of them knew him, and knew he was a miser, and that he had been the means of sending a great many good man off to the war, and breaking up their homes and claiming their property. One of the boys took a pair of pinchers[1] from his pocket and took hold of the old man's hand and told him if he did not tell where his money was that he would pull out his finger nails. The old man tried to pull his hand away say again he had no money.

I stood over the bed looking at this barbarous action but could say nothing to prevent it least they should turn on me. They asked him again telling him they would cut him in pieces if you did not tell. The old miser again said that he had none. The one that had the pinchers took the old man's hand again and pulled out two nails, and then asked him again. The old man cried with pain and still said he had no money. The finger nail business was carried on until all his finger nails were gone and asking him every time they pulled a nail for his money, and all the old man said was no. He cried and begged of them not to kill him for he had no money. His hands

---

1 Federhen is probably referring to the tool called "pincers" in modern usage.

were bleeding and he was growing very weak for he had not much blood to lose.

While three of us stayed in the room with the old man the others went searching the house to find the treasure pulling up all the planks and looking in every hole and corner. At last one of the boys sung out here it is, I found it. The old man tried to raise his head to look but he was too weak to move. He gave a groan and then closed his eyes. He was most gone.

We all ran to see the treasure. One of the boys had pulled up a plank in the rear of the cabin and under it was a large stone, and there lay a box about two foot square and was most full of gold and silver coins. Each of us filled our pockets and put the rest in a bag and tied it onto one of the saddles. After this we went into the house to look at the old man. He lay motionless.

They covered him so that the blood would not show and we left the house.

24

Battle Between Quantrill's Men and Confederate Regulars

WE TOOK another road to go to camp which was much longer way than we had come. We had rode about five miles when we came in sight of some men coming towards us. We halted to see how many there were. There were only five and the boys said they could clean them out in a very few moments, if they did not get out of their way.

We rode on as we came nearer I could see them fixing their rifles as if ready for an attack. One of the boys said they were some of Gen. McCallough's scouts and it would not do for them to go past the old man's house, for then we should be detected and followed up by other scouts so the best thing we can do is to attack them and drive them back on to another road, so the order was be ready at any moment.

We rode on a little further and now we were within pistol shot of them. One of the boys while fixing his revolver accidentally discharged one of the barrels. The scouts thinking we had commenced the attack, leveled their rifles and gave us a volley. One of the boys was wounded in the arm and my horse received a slight flesh wound in his fore shoulder. Before they would reload their pieces we put spurs to our horses and dashed forward upon the scouts firing a volley at them as we advanced. They turned their horses and started on a double quick. We followed close behind them shooting and killing one of their number. He fell in the road and his horse along with his companions kept on at a rapid rate.

We did not chase them any further, but stopped to see who the dying reb was. He had been shot through the bowels and groaned piteously. He said he belong to Gen. McCallough's scouts and they were out looking up deserters. He was almost dead and could not answer any more questions. The boys took his revolver and rifle away from him and then pulled him off into the woods and left him there to die, and we rode off not seeing anything more of the scouts.

It was quite late before we reached camp, so we put our horses out to graze, and then boiled some chickens for supper. After supper we counted our money and gave a share of it to the Captain who always came in for a share of the spoils.

25

LIFE IN QUANTRILL'S CAMP

IT WAS my night to stand guard and I did not like my job. I took a rifle and my two revolvers and went just outside the camp so that I could overlook the camp and horses and I would not be relieved until midnight. I had my pipe and tobacco with me so I worried out the time smoking.

This was not what I enlisted into the Federal Army for to stand guard for the rebs or to connect myself with them in any way, but what was I to do, for my own safety I must stay with them until I could find the direct course to go to reach the federal lines. I spoke to them several times about my going but they told me I had better not try it yet for the country was full of scouts, and if old McCullough had me again he might use me a little rough. They told me I could stay with them as long as I wished and when I was ready to go, they would help me off and give me the best directions. I made myself contented with this, and all my leisure time I was learning some to read and write.[1]

Sometimes I would go out with them on a scout, but I was getting tired of this way of living, and wished myself back in the army, but the nearest point that I could reach in safety was about three hundred miles from where I was. This I would have to travel on foot, for it would be impossible to

---

1 In other words, Federhen was teaching others to read and write.

travel along the roads on horseback without being picked up by scouts. At times I was almost discouraged and thought the best thing that I could do was to stay where I was, and make myself as comfortable as possible until the war was over. I was having a good time and nothing to do, a good horse to ride and plenty to eat. What could I ask for more then this only to be inside the federal lines.

The boys did not only plunder and kill the union people, but where ever they found in old rebel who had money or a good horse they always made him give it up. All they wanted was money and did not care where or how they got it, so when ever they made a raid on a rebel, I was with them to see the fun, for I was getting used to it.

I had been with them about six weeks witnessing there villainous actions such as killing and hanging men and women when one afternoon about four o'clock some of the boys who had been out on a scout, came into the camp and wanted us to come out into a little piece of wood a little away from camp to see them perform a surgical operation. About a dozen of the boys and myself went to see what was up. When we reach the woods, we found some of the boys there, with a negro man bound hand and foot his hands tied behind him. He was a stout good looking Negro, weighing about one hundred and eighty pounds. They threw him down on the grass and then drove stakes into the ground, one on each side of his neck and the same with his feet and then tied him fast, so that he could not move, or raise either head hands or feet. They been cut and tore off his clothes.

This may seem to my readers to be a story and not the truth, but as I said at the beginning of my writings that these were undisputable facts in such actions not only happened once, but about every day. This was the only one of the kind that I had witness and hoped it would be the last.

After the negro was securely bound one of the boys took a knife from his pocket, with the remarks, now boys we will see what this nigger is made of. He was tortured in several unmanly ways at first. He lay there screaming and groaning filling the forest, with a frightful echo. There next movement was to cut open his bowels, and one of the boys (or more rightfully named the brutes) who had on a pair of gloves pulled his innards out and lay them on the grass. This put the poor fellow out of misery, for I pitied him, but did not dare to say or do a thing myself. He was bleeding at a fearful rate, and his eyes looked like two balls of fire. The next thing they done was to cut from his collar bone, down through his ribs. They then took out his heart liver and lungs and lay them on the ground. They then cut off his head and stuck it on a stake. Some dug a hole, and put his carcass into it and covered it over with dirt, placing the stake with the head on it at the head of the hole. We left this place and went back to camp.

It was getting quite late, and it was my night to stand guard. After supper I went to my post to worry out half the night, and every stump of a tree I saw I imagined it was a negro. Midnight came and with it came my relief. I was tired and as soon as I was into my bed, I went fast asleep.

26

DEPARTURE FROM QUANTRILL'S CAMP

IN THE morning after I had eaten my breakfast, I told the Captain and some of the boys that I had a notion of leaving them and try my luck in getting back again to the federal lines. They said I had better give up at the notion and stay with them, and share with them in the prizes. I thank them and told them that I would rather run my chances in getting back to the federal lines where I belong. They said they did not blame me for that but they would like to have me stay with them. I had learnt several to read and write and they felt sorry to have me leave them. I stayed in camp all that day cooking crackers and stripping beef to get ready for my journey, for I was going to start the next day.[1]

That night the Captain called me into his tent and gave me the best directions he knew for me to travel by. At the same time he gave me a small revolver, and tell me I had better leave my large ones, for they would be heavy to carry. I sat up quite late that night talking with the boys, the most of them wishing they could go with me to the north. In the morning everything was already. I had a suit of rebel uniform on and a belt strapped around me which held two bags of gold, and my revolver besides a haversack field with hard

1 A cracker was a small hard biscuit, named for the sound it made when broken. To strip, in this sense, is to skin a carcass. Bartlett, *Dictionary of Americanisms*, 96; *Oxford English Dictionary.*

crackers and dried beef. After everything was all ready I lay down and went to sleep and slept until late in the afternoon, for I was to start the evening.

After supper the boys came out of their tents to shake hands and bade me good bye and told them that if ever any of them were placed in my situation inside the federal lines and I could do anything to help them, that I would do it. Some of the boys walked down the road with me for some ways then bid me good bye and went back to camp.

27

Recaptured by
Confederates Again

I AM alone again to travel through the strange country at night. My only compass was the stars and wind. I travelled that night and slept the next day. The next night I travelled keeping about half a mile from the Red River. [1]

In the morning I lay down in the brush and slept until about noon. It was very pleasant and as I had been traveling along the road the most of the way, and not seeing or hearing from any body I thought it would be safe for me to travel along the road by day so that my journey would sooner be to an end. I ate a cracker and a piece of beef and felt quite strong and started off. I had traveled about two hours, when I saw it in the road ahead of me and about a mile and a half away, some mounted men coming towards me on the double quick. As soon as I see them I started on the run through the woods towards the river. [2] As soon as I turned one of them discharged his rifle at me but I was out of range. The river was about half mile from the road and I must get to it before they

---

1 It is not clear if Federhen is traveling on the north or south bank of the Red River. He is heading generally east from an unknown point at least 25 miles northeast of Bonham.

2 Federhen is probably returning to the Red River.

come upon me. I ran so fast as I could, leaving my haversack and food behind me.

When I got to the river I heard the horses breaking through the timber. My only chance now was to jump into the river, and run my chances of being shot in the river. Not being a good swimmer there was as much chance of my drowning as of being shot. I took my revolver and held it in my mouth, unstrapped my belt, and threw it money and all into the river, so if they got me, they would not get the money. The river was low so I climb down the bank, and jumping in, I struck out for the other side.

I was about half way across when the horseman came in site on the banks. They shouted to me to stop and come back, or they would shoot. They were about twenty five yards below where I jumped from. They fired, each a shot gate a buzz and splashed into the river over my head. In my excitement I dropped my pistol, and it sank to the bottom of the river. I soon gained the opposite side and climbed up its banks. As I was climbing up they fired several pistol shots at me. I gained the bank and started into the brush. I ran for about a mile and lay down under some brush and listened to see if I could hear anything from them.

I lay there until night and the next day until sunset when I feeling rather hungry, and wishing to continue my journey. I started out of my hiding place. I thought the safest way for me to go was to go west, and keep away from the river, for the river might be guarded. So with out any baggage, I started out of the woods. I had not traveled far before I came to an open space in a road. I looked both up and down the road, but could not see any signs of horses or man. It has begun to grow dark so I ventured out on to the road. I had not traveled a dozen yards before I heard a rifle shot, and before I could turn around to see where it came from, the bullet buzzed passed my head. I turned to see what my chances were in getting to the woods, but there was none, for a horseman was coming towards me at a rapid pace with his revolver in his hand shouting for me to halt. I see there was no other chance so I halted and told him I would surrender.

As he rode up to me, he asked if I had a pistol or knife about me, and if I had I had better give them up. He halted about three yards from me, and told me if I came towards him he would blow my brains out. He kept me standing there about fifteen minutes when two horseman rode up both from different directions. As they came up one of them said that he reckoned they could starve me out if they stayed there a week. They did not ask me to what I belonged, for they supposed I was a deserter from the rebel army. They marched me in front of them until it was quite late and then stopped at a house for the rest of the night. To secure me they tied me both hands and feet, and I lay on the floor, and slept a little that night.

In the morning I was released from my rope and they gave me a little piece of corn bread and dried beef. After they had eaten their breakfast they mounted their horses and we continued our journey. I knew from the direction they were going they were going to Gen. McCallough's head quarters. I asked one of the men and he said they were going to Barnum to give me up for a deserter. I told them that I was not a deserter and would not belong to the rebel army for my life. I am a federal soldier, and I am not ashamed nor afraid to tell you or the whole rebel army. They laughed at me and said that I could not play that, for it would not make it go any easier for me, for they knew I was a deserter, and if they had any suspicion of mine being a Yankee, they would hang me to the first tree they came to. I thought the least said on that question the better for me.

They traveled me that day and the next until we got within about eight miles of Barnum when they stopped to rest for the night. I watched every opportunity to make my escape, but they kept a close watch over me.

In the morning we marched towards Barnum. We reached it about noon, when I came inside of Gen' head quarters, and knew that I should have to face the Gen. and other officers who knew me, I felt as a man feels when he has his sentence of death. I did not expect to see the Stars & Stripes again. As soon we came to the door of the Gen.'s head quarters the guard dismounted their horses and brought me before the Gen. followed by several of the officers who were standing in the hall and who recognized me. The Gen. and his adjutant were all alone in the room when we entered, but before we had been there five minutes the hall was filled with officers and men, the most of them I do not believe ever saw a Yankee before, for they were looking, and asking one another, which the Yankee was.

As soon as the old Gen' saw me, he exclaimed, What you brought that cussed Yankee back again. Why did you not leave him where you caught him. One of the guard said that he would if he had been sure of his being a Yankee, but he thought I was a deserter, trying to get back to the Yankee lines. The Gen' asked me a great many questions about where I had been, and about Quantralls men, but I did not give him any satisfaction. He kept me there sometime exhibiting me to the crowd who used anything but flattering remarks on me. This did not trouble me in the least, for I had got used to it, as I had in going without anything to eat. The Gen' wrote a few lines on a slip of paper and handed it to an officer, who was standing by, telling him to take me and put me in the guard house. After he had fulfilled his orders, then looking at me he said, I have had trouble enough with you, and as soon as I can hear from Camp Ford I shall know what to do with you. This was much better than what I expected, and I thought as long as there was life there was hope.

28

IMPRISONED AGAIN IN BONHAM

THEY MARCHED me out of the Gen's head quarters towards a small log cabin, with a sign over the top, printed in rustic letters Blacksmith's Shop. There were soldiers standing about the door and I was much surprised and curious to know what they were taking me there for.

As soon as I got under the shelter my curiosity was soon made known. The officer read his orders to the blacksmith, who went looking over some iron rings, and soon found a pair that he thought would fit me. He then told me to put my foot on the anvil so that he could measure my ankles. He got my measure and then began to make them. He took four half round pieces of iron and riveted them together so that they made two rings. Then he took a bar of iron about eighteen inches long and fastened the ring onto each end of it and then riveted to the rings around my ankles. He then took the chain about two foot long, and fastened it in the center of this bar, and attached to the end of the chain was a twenty pound ball.

I asked the officer if there was not anything else he could put on my foot. The officer looked at me as if he wanted to knock me over and said that he would take some of the Yankee independence out before he got through with me, and if I said anything more that he would iron my hands after my irons were fastened.

They marched me off towards the guardhouse, which was about a quarter of a mile from head quarters. I found it very difficult about walking for my feet were spread eighteen inches apart, and had to pull the ball after me. We got to the guard house after a while and there I found about thirty confederate prisoners, about all whom were as myself, for they had been captured trying to get to the federal lines, and had been put in there to await their sentence.

The guardhouse was about thirty foot deep, and fifteen foot wide, and a fireplace at one end, and the door at the other, outside was a yard about a quarter of an acre large, and this was stockaded in by long logs set into the ground and pointed at the top so that it was impossible to get over them. There were about twenty guards guarding the place, and the water they had to drink had to be carried a quarter of a mile in buckets. The guards opened the gate and let me into the yard. The prisoners were wondering who that poor fellow was, and the reason they had ironed him so heavy.

I went into the house and sat down on the floor. I was tired, and the irons were cutting my ankles so that they were bleeding. The prisoners soon found out who I was and came into the house, and began asking me all manner of questions. I told him I was to tired to talk much and told them to wait until morning. They wanted to know if I was hungry. I said I was, so they went to work and cooked a piece of meat, and baked a corn cake for me. I ate them with a good relish, for they tasted to me better than the finest dinner I had ever eaten.

This was one of the prisoners who I noticed when I first entered the yard. He did not look like a southern or western man. His manner and talk showed he had had a good education, and the thought passed through my mind that he was a eastern man. He was the first and only one who offered me his blankets to lay on, and at night he tied a wet cloth around my ankles and slept with me under his blankets.

The next morning I felt much better but my ankles were lame and sore. My friend who I had slept with and had been so kind got me my blankets and examined the irons to see if there was any possible way to get them off so to rest my feet, but they were fastened on too firm. I had been there several days before I asked him where he was from, and if he had not been educated in the east. He said that he was a Union man as much as I was, and that he was from Philadelphia, and at the breaking out of the war he was in Texas and was forced into the rebel army, and that he had made several efforts to get back into the federal lines but without success.

I asked what the prisoners called him doctor for. He said that that was his profession and he had studied for it in Philadelphia. I told him I had an Uncle in that city who was a physician and asked him if he knew any by the name which I gave him.[1] He grasped me by the hand, and said, is he your Uncle, why I was one of his students and a better or dearer friend I never had. I wasn't as much rejoice at this as was my friend, for I was sure as long as I was with him that I had a friend.

I had been there a week when my right ankle began to show signs of scurvy where the iron had torn the flesh off and my ankle was very much swollen.[2] I spoke to the guard, and asked them to tell the Gen' that the irons my ankles were tearing the flesh so that it was impossible for me to step on my feet and ask him if he would not remove them. They carried the message. The answer I received was, no matter if they tear your feet off, then we are sure you will not run away

---

1 Federhen's mother was born Elizabeth Brooks. There is a Silas S. Brooks, M.D., listed in an 1864 Philadelphia city directory. According to the 1870 census, Silas was born in Massachusetts in 1817, making him a possible uncle to Oscar Federhen. *McElroy's Philadelphia City Directory for 1864* (Philadelphia: E. C. & J. Biddle & Co., 1864), xxxiv.

2 Scurvy is caused by a deficiency of vitamin C, and its symptoms can include joint pain. Schroeder-Lein, *Encyclopedia of Civil War Medicine*, 271–73.

again. I thanked the guard and told him to give my compliments to the Gen'.

My friend, Dr. Upshaw, for that was his name, kept cold water on them and in time it took the swelling down.[3] The chain that held the ball was a common link chain, and the doctor and several of the prisoners had been trying to spread one of the links so that I could take the ball off. They succeeded in spreading one of them, but I wore it the most of the time for fear of being seen by the guard. I only thought if I could get one of the rings over my ankle that I should be all right, and would try my chances in getting away again.

The swelling had all gone, and I tried to get the ring off but it almost pulled my foot off. The doctor took a piece of hard wood and stretched the ring several times so that it sprung it together, and by soaking and rubbing soap on my heel and instep, I managed to slip it off, but not without tearing the flesh from the top of my foot. I had got it off and how was I to get it on again. I did not want it on again for my feet felt much easier without them on, than they did when they were spread eighteen inches apart.

I kept them off two days but I had to stay in the house, with my feet covered up with a blanket playing off sick. One of the boys had sprung the ring in such a shape that by soaking my heel and straightening my foot, I could slip it off or on, but on the other foot I could not stir the ring. I was quite comfortable now for nights I could take them off, and by day time I would wear them. My ankle was a complete wreck. The flesh was about all off and the joints were as visible as if there had never been any flesh on them, and I feared I might lose my foot. I kept wet cloths on it all the time and kept it as quiet as possible, so that when I had the irons off it fell quite easy.

---

3 No one by this name is listed in census or city directory records as a physician living in Philadelphia during this period.

I had been there about two weeks, when not only myself but also prisoners found fault with the water they had to drink, and spoke to the officers of the guard about it, but all the answer we received was, it is good enough for you'es to drink.[4] It kept growing worse and soon some of them at head quarters drank it and made them sick, so they went to work and searched the well and found an infant child about a week old, and had been in the well about three weeks.

They did not give us any more of that water for a wonder.

---

4 Usually rendered as "you'uns," this serves in some Southern varieties of English as the second person plural.

29

A Second Escape
from Bonham

I WAS getting tired of my new home and wanted a change, so I spoke to the Doctor and asked what he thought of our making our escape. He said he was ready and when ever I said the word he was ready. I told him that it would be better if all in the guard house would make a break, but we must be careful who we speak to about it for fear it might get outside, and then that would shorten our sentence if they heard of it at headquarters.

The Doctor and myself used every precaution in speaking to the prisoners about it, and all we spoke to was in favor of it. We had spoken to about twenty of the boys, and the others knew nothing about it. Two of the boys lived about 3 miles from head quarters and knew the lay of the country, but they all wanted to know how I was going with my ball and chains. I told them not to fret about me, but to be ready when I spoke to them and be sure and not say a word about it to anyone if they wanted to make it a success of it.

The third week had very near expired, and I thought it a good time to try my luck. It had been raining all day and it was cloudy in the evening. I spoke to the Doctor and told him that this was the night for us to make our escape. Every night at dark they shut and locked us up in the guard house and put two guards over us, one in front and the other at the rear of the house, and outside the stockade there were four guards, one on each side. The door of the guard house was fastened by a hook and staple, and the gate was fastened with a bolt on the outside.

After they had locked us in for the night, I went around and told the boys to be ready at my call for I was going to make a break that night. The call was Halo Bob and be ready at midnight. I cautioned every man not to wear anything that was white, and not to carry any baggage with him. They were all ready at any time, so the Doctor and myself lay down to get a little sleep. I took the iron ball off and laid it at the head of my bed. I next got the iron ring off my right ankle, but could not get it off the other. I tore off a piece of blanket which answered for a rope and tied the bar and ring up against my left leg so that it was out of the way, but did not feel very comfortable.

I slept until near midnight, when I woke everything was quiet in the house, and the guard were having a social chat on their beats. I rose to my feet to look out a crack in the door to see what the weather was, and I could not have selected a better night, dark and cloudy. I had no more than touched my feet to the floor, before every man's head was up and ready for the start. I held up my hand in motion for them to lye still. I then spoke to the Doctor and told him I was ready. He was on his feet in an instant.

I looked through the crack of the door and saw the guard pass. I had a case knife in my hand, the blade of which I slipped through the crack so that it rested on the hook.[1] I turned and spoke in a loud whisper to the boys to make

---

1 The door was equipped with a "hook and eye" latch, which is a length of thick wire with a hook on one end and a loop on the other. The loop is stapled to the sash, and the hook is run through an eyelet screwed into the door. When the door is cracked open, the hook spans the gap and prevents the door from opening any further. Augustine C. Passmore, *Handbook of Technical Terms Used in Architecture and Building and their Allied Trades and Subjects* (New York: D. Van Nostrand, 1904), 181.

ready. They were all to their feet in an instant. Every nerve in my system was trembling, not from fear but from excitement, for life or death was now before me in my comrades. I well knew if ever I was recaptured again that death would be my only chance, so with a club, which I had saved from the fire wood, I was determined not to be recaptured again alive.

Always ready and the Doctor at my side, I watched for the guard to pass the door, and then gave the call Halo Bob in at the same time lifting the hook and pushing the door open. The Doctor and myself both jumped from the house followed by twenty or more of the boys. We had no sooner than touched the ground before the guard that were inside fired at us, the bullet passed through the Doctors hat and missing mine. I made for the gate and try to open it, but it was fastened, not only with a bolt but with a hook at the top. I hallowed to the boys to pull the gate down for I knew this was our only chance. They got hold, and in half a minute the gate was lying on the ground, but not until after the guards were aroused from their slumbers, and were outside of their quarters firing into us, shouting to us to go back, or they would kill everyone of us. I hallowed to the boys to follow me, but some of them started off in the opposite direction, and the Doctor was amongst the number.

I kept on and was followed by a number of the boys. When I had got to the rear of the guard house I met two guards. They both leveled their guns and fired. A poor little fellow who was trying to make his escape and keeping as close to me as he could was shot and found dead beside me. Several shots were fired at random through the woods, but no more was heard from them that night. We ran for about a mile, when we stopped and I counted the boys. There were fourteen of us, and what ever became of the Doctor I could not say.

The two boys that lived close by was with us and they led the way. There was a large opening in the river about five miles below, and an island in the center with thick brush and trees. This river is called the Bardark River and is a low swampy place. We reached the island before daylight and made a raft out of some drift logs, and crossed over to the island. We then destroyed the log so that no trace was left and went into the brush.

We laid there all day keeping a lookout for the scouts. About four o'clock there rode six of the scouts by the island looking for traces, and looking towards the island, they found no trace and passed on down the river, and went back again about sunset. This is all we see of the scouts while I was with them.

That night the two boys that live close by, or about two miles from where we now were went home and brought back two double barrel shot guns, some corn bread, and about half a bushel of corn. This was gratefully received, for we were all hungry. One of the boys took an old file from his pocket and handed it to me to file my irons off. I was not long about it, and I could I assure you they felt much easier.

30

TRAVEL TO SHREVEPORT

I KNEW it was wasting time for me to stop on the island so I made up my mind to go alone and start towards Shreveport, La. The distance I did not exactly know but I reckon it was about six hundred miles or more for me to travel.[1] I told the boys that I was going to leave them and wanted to go alone. I gave them my reasons. I told them that they were all at home in their own country, for most of them lived in Texas and Missouri, and my course was in a different direction, for I was going to travel towards Shreveport.[2]

I stayed with them four days, and in the morning of the fourth day before daylight one of the boys that had come from his home brought with him a mule with a nice saddle and bridle all ready to mount. He tied the mule to a tree in the woods and crossed to the island. I was asleep when he came. He woke me, and said if I was going, that he had a mule in the woods, and I was welcome to it. I did not wait until daylight, but dressed myself with what extra clothing I had, shook hands with what boys there were awake, bid them good bye and started across the river with my comrade to get the mule.

---

1 Overland, Shreveport is about 160 miles from Bonham.

2 Until Jun. 6, 1865, Shreveport was still controlled by Confederate troops. Perry Anderson Snyder, "Shreveport, Louisiana, during the Civil War and Reconstruction," Ph.D. dissertation, Florida State University (1979), 134.

They all wished me good luck and if ever I reached the federal lines they could think I was the smartest Yankee they ever heard of.

I thought I would be the luckiest fellow out if ever I succeeded in getting through to the federal lines, but I feared my chances were but few.

31

REMINISCENCES OF COMANCHES AT BONHAM

THE SECOND week that I was at Barnum guard house, a tribe of Comanche Indians came into the town and made a treaty with Gen. McCullough to buy arms and ammunition.[1] They brought a white woman with them, which they had captured on the frontiers about eight years before, and had been living with their Chief. This woman they sold to Gen. McCullough, for lead, powder and whiskey, and for the privilege of going down into the Boardark River bottom to cut timber for bows and arrows. This was granted.

They stayed in town about four days, and every day they would pass the guard house in going to the river. They were an ugly filthy looking class both men and women. Evenings when they came from the river every man and woman was loaded with Boardark timber. They were laying in a good stock. One day some of them stopped at the guard house to trade. I had a confederate jacket on which I had got from

---

1 By this period, almost all Comanches lived "on a strip between the Arkansas and Canadian Rivers" in Indian Territory more than 130 miles from Bonham, although some lived in the Choctaw territory immediately across the Red River from Bonham. Pekka Hämäläinen, *The Comanche Empire* (New Haven: Yale University Press, 2008), 311–12.

Quantralls camp. One of the Indians fell in love with it and offered me his blanket for it. I exchanged with him, but on examining it found it full of live stock. I picked them off and cleaned it, and I found it much more convenient than my jacket would have been. I carried it when I broke guard and have it now in my possession keeping it as a relic of the Comanche Indians of Texas.

32

FURTHER TRAVELS
TOWARD SHREVEPORT

I WAS soon across the river and found the mule tied to the tree where are my friend had left him. I mounted, bid my friend good bye and started off. I made my mule go as fast as I could keeping on the road so as to make the best of my time.

About noon I met two horsemen on the road. I halted and ask them where they were going. They said they were going to Sherman. They asked where I was going. I told them I was a carrier from Gen. McCallough, on my way to Shreveport with dispatches. They asked me what the news was. I told them that the Gen' had made a treaty with the Comanche Indians, and that there was a great many prisoners in the guard house, and they had caught a Yankee spying around head quarters and were going to hang him. I told them that was all the news I knew anything about, and that I was in a hurry for I had orders to go as quickly as possible. I bid them good bye and galloped off.

I rode on until it began to grow dark when I stopped at a house to get something to eat, for I had not eaten anything since the night before. There was an old man and woman in the house, and they got me up a good supper of corn bread and bacon. I told them that I was a carrier and I must go a few miles further that night. My mule was tired and while I was eating my supper the old man had given him some fodder, so that both of mule and my self felt much better. I think the old man and woman for their kindness bid them good bye and rode off.

I rode all night and the next day until sunset when my mule began to grow tired, and I knew that he was about done for, for I had rode him hard and fast. He had fallen down on his knees twice, so I dismounted, took off saddle and bridle, laid them at the foot of a tree and let the mule go, for I knew that he would soon be picked up. I started on foot to travel the rest of the way, I was hungry and knowing it would be dangerous to be seen, for they all knew that a carrier had no business to be without a horse, so I must keep in the woods and travel by night the rest of my time.

All that I had to eat until I reached Shrevesport was wild onions and sassafras root, with two ears of corn which I had found in the road. It was about two weeks before I came to Shrevesport, and what my fate was there I did not know. I had got within about five miles of the city when I saw a negro in the field at work. I called to him and he wanted to know what I wanted. I told him I wished to speak to him a moment. He came to where I was, and I told him my story and asked him if he could get me something to eat. I told him I was a Yankee and was trying to get back into the federal lines. The negro began to laugh and said why yous all right. De Yankees has a whipped de South all to nothing and we expect them here every day. I asked the negro if he was honest in what he said. He said he was and dat Lee an old guff had runed away.

I asked him if there was many soldiers in the city. He said there was heaps of them and I might go into the city and every body would think I was a rebel, for I was dressed in rebel uniform and had my blanket, for the most of them carried a blanket. The negro said if I would wait he would get me something to eat. He went to his cabin and soon returned with some corn bread and a piece of bacon. I thank him for it and started off into the woods again to have a good square meal.

33

EMBARKING ON A STEAMBOAT TOWARDS FEDERAL LINES

(MAY 31, 1865)

I STAYED there all night and in the morning I washed myself, brushed my clothes, so as to look as respectable as possible, threw my blanket over my shoulder and started towards the city. I met a great many rebel soldiers, but they all minded their own business and I kept on into the city, and I looked as much like a reb as any of them. I stopped into the city all day, and at night I went into the woods to sleep. There were about four divisions of troops in and about the city.

The next day I went to the city and joined in with some rebs who were going to draw rations of tobacco and bacon. The weed that I had learnt to love so much as food, and a great many times it answered the purpose of food, for I could eat it like sweet cakes. I passed for a reb up all that day drawing my rations of bacon and tobacco, and being amongst them with my eyes and ears both open to see and hear all that was going on.

In the afternoon as I was going down Texas Street,[1] that being the principle street in the city and where Gen' Kerby Smith[2] had his head quarters. I saw a notice posted on the door of the Gen's quarters, stating that the steamer *Lafonche* was to go down the river the next day at ten o'clock under the flag of truce, to meet the federal fleet.[3] The fare was forty dollars in gold. There was quite a number of the rebs who were buying their tickets so as to get there parole from the federals as soon as they met them and then continue down the river to New Orleans where a number of them lived.

I stayed around the head quarters until quite late, hoping I might pick up a ticket, but those that had them kept them in a safe place. I went back into the woods to sleep that night but my mind was too busy to sleep, planning some way to get onto the boat and secure myself so as to get down the river and not be seen. Before daylight I was at the wharf watching my chances.

The wharf was full of boxes, old furniture, baskets and two carriages. They had about a dozen negros at work loading the steamer, and a white man as overseer. They were getting the carriages on the upper deck and were hoisting it up by

1 Texas Street was the main business district in nineteenth-century Shreveport. It runs perpendicular to the bank of the Red River. Snyder, "Shreveport, Louisiana, During the Civil War and Reconstruction," 46.

2 Edmund Kirby Smith commanded the Trans-Mississippi Department from 1863 until the end of the war. Between Apr. 24, 1864, and May 20, 1865, his headquarters were in Shreveport. Jeffrey S. Prushankin, *A Crisis in Confederate Command: Edmund Kirby Smith, Richard Taylor, and the Army of the Trans-Mississippi* (Baton Rouge: Louisiana State University Press, 2005), 29, 213.

3 A steamship named the *Lafourche* plied the Louisiana rivers during this period. On May 31, 1865, it departed Shreveport "with a large number of refugees on their way home," and on Jun. 6, 1865, it docked in New Orleans, having come "in from Red River last evening, and appear[ing] to be in a bad condition." Shreveport *Semi-Weekly News*, Jun. 6, 1865: 2; New Orleans *Times*, Jun. 7, 1865: 8, retrieved from newspapers.com.

ropes. I asked the overseer if he wanted any help and if he did that I would help him. He told me to go and help those niggers get those carriages on the upper deck. I got hold of the rope, and flew around making myself useful helping the negros load the goods off the wharf. They were storing things down the hole through the hatch.

I was helping the overseer to tie the rope around the goods so as to lower them down the hole. We were lowering furniture and the overseer told me to get down the hole and show the nigger how to store the goods. I was not long going down and soon put things to rights. I came on deck again and began helping the negros to load. I threw my blanket and a small piece of bacon, which I had tied up in my blanket, on a woodpile as high as I could get it. It was now about time for the boat to start, and they have not got quite loaded.

While the overseers back was turned, I jumped down the hole and began to help the negroes put things away, and to look for a hiding place for myself. I went out towards the stern of the boat and found a ladder which led on deck just behind the engine. I went up and looked around, all hands were on the front helping to load. Wood was piled as high as they could pile all over the deck and I picked out my hiding place in a very few moments. I climbed over the wood until I got to the top and then lay down between it and the upper deck. I did not lay there long before the fireman began to throw in wood, and I heard him say that they were going to start in half an hour.[4]

Soon I heard the call of the Captain telling every one to leave the boat, negroes and all, and they that had tickets, come one by one and give up your tickets. The boat was searched to see if all had left the boat, but they did not find

---

4 The fireman tended the furnace of the steamship. *Oxford English Dictionary.*

poor yank on top of the wood pile. In half an hour the boat was pushed off.

I crawled up close to the bow of the boat so that I might hear the conversation of the passengers. They were rebs all of them, and if they had known that a Yankee was so close to them they would have thrown me into the river. I lay there that day wishing I had my blanket or rather the bacon for I was hungry. It was getting dark and I ventured to look over the woodpile and there I saw my blanket where I had left it.

34

A Steamboat Trip
Down the Red River

THERE WAS a great many Confederate soldiers onboard going down the river to meet the Yanks and get their parole.[1] They all looked the same as myself, and I knew that all on board had paid their fares, and I was determined to go on deck before morning.

Midnight came, there was quite a number walking on deck. Some were singing, others were talking and laughing and a few laying asleep about the deck. I crept over to where I had got onto the pile of wood. The engineer had been using some, and as soon as I begin to climb down the wood begin to fall, and down came yank and wood in a hurry, making a great noise, which brought the engineer to see what the matter was, and want to know what I was doing on that pile of wood.[2] I told him I was trying to get up to the top, so as to lay

---

1 The Confederates had already surrendered all of Louisiana to Union forces on Jun. 2. Kirby Smith vacated Shreveport on May 20, but Union forces did not occupy the city until Jun. 6. Order was maintained by a contingent of Missouri troops who did not follow Kirby Smith out of town. Prushankin, *A Crisis in Confederate Command*, 214; Snyder, "Shreveport, Louisiana, During the Civil War and Reconstruction," 134.

2 In this sense, the engineer oversaw the steam engine onboard. *Oxford English Dictionary*.

down and have a nap and the wood fell back on me. He told me to get out of this and not try it again.

I went out on deck thinking how luckily I had got out of that scrape. I went and got my blanket, I took the piece of bacon and soon devoured it, and then lay down on my blanket and slept amongst my rebel companions for the rest of the night. In the morning I went around deck the same as any of them and made myself as comfortable as I could. There was some negroes on board employed in carrying wood and cleaning up the boat. Each soldier had to find his own food, but the officers messed together in the cabin.[3] What was left from the officers cabin came to the negroes, and while the negroes were eating their food I would hang around them, and if they had anything left, I would beg it of them. Sometimes they would save me a little, I was very grateful to them for I was a poor hungry yank.

Everything went off quiet well that day, the boat having a confederate flag at the mast. Towards evening I went up into the cabin, the officers were playing cards and having a good time. At one end of the cabin there hung two confederate flags and under these flags the officers were playing. I went back on deck and lay down hoping that that would be the last night, I should sleep under the confederate flag.

The next morning we met several steamboats which had been drove up the river and who were concealing themselves in small streams, for they were loaded with cotton, and they said they would burn it before they would let the Yankees have it. There were several marked batteries along the river, and every one we came to the boat would stop and report. Towards evening they had a general cleaning up on the boat, the deck was washed the wood picked up, and all on board were trying to look as well as possible. They took down their

---

3 To mess was to eat in a group. Wright, *The Language of the Civil War*, 190.

confederate flags, and in their place they hoisted the flag of truce, and I knew by their actions they were nearing the federal fleet. I kept awake all night watching for the fleet but there was no sign of them.

In the morning a courier passed along the banks. He was hailed by the officer of the boat who asked us how far the Yankees were down the river. He replied that they were at Alexandria about five miles below.[4] I thought this was the best news I had ever heard. I went and sat on the bow of the boat so that I might be one of the first to see the Yankees. The engine put on more steam so that the boat might go faster, and I was watching more eagerly for the stars and stripes. Every time the boat rounded a bend, I would imagine I could see my native flag.

It was not much more than an hour before we came in sight of the fleet, and forgetting myself, and where I was, I jumped up clapping my hands and shouting three cheers for the American flag. I had no more than got the words out of my mouth, before I received a kick followed by the remarks that if I did that again that they would drown me. That soon brought me to my senses.

---

4 Alexandria is on the Red River about 112 miles (as the crow flies) downstream from Shreveport.

35

ENCOUNTERING THE UNION ARMY

(BETWEEN JUNE 2 AND JUNE 6, 1865)

I COULD see less than two dozen flags before me, and every one looked like a nation. As soon as the boat had got within a hundred yards of the fleet a signal was fired by the gun boat for the *Lafuche* to lay by. She replied with this order and when she pulled along side of the bank for the officers to get off, I jumped from the bow towards the shore, but lighted in the river. I soon got out of the water.

The Captain of the boat hallowed to me to stop, and not go on shore for he had orders, not to let any one off the boat until he had reported to commanding officers. I paid no attention to what he said but climbed up the bank assisted by some soldiers who were standing there. I spoke to an officer that was standing there and told him that I was a Union soldier and I had come down on the boat from Shrevesport and wished to see the commanding officer before the boat landed. He started off with me towards Gen' Herrons head-quarters.[1] I turned to see if the boat had landed but there stood the

---

1 Francis Jay Herron was the Union general in command of the Northern District of Louisiana; on Jun. 2, he had established his headquarters at Alexandria, and moved to Shreveport on Jun. 6. "Major General F. J. Herron," *Annals of Iowa* 5, no. 1 (Jan. 1867): 806; New Orleans *Times-Democrat*, Jun. 6, 1865: 4, retrieved from newspapers.com; Shreveport *Semi-Weekly News*, Jun. 10, 1865: 2, retrieved from newspapers.com.

Captain and his clerks looking at me in amazement while some of the boys on shore were singing out, well I reckon you have had a yank on board and did not know it. I soon reached the Gen' boat. The Gen's orderly reported to him. I was shown into the cabin. The Gen' wanted to know who I was, and if I was a federal soldier, where and what I did belong to. Well he might ask those questions, for I looked worse than any reb. My clothes were torn and full of dirt and vermin, for they had not been off for about four weeks. My hair had grown wild and hung in a tangled mass over my shoulders. My face was covered with a fine beard and dirt and my complexion was dark from exposure. No flesh on my bones, and my eyes settled in my head. I was a picture of what you might call a living skeleton.

I answered his questions, told him about the flags which they had hoisted the first few days, about the cotton boats and about the masked batteries along the river. I also gave him all the information I knew concerning Shreveport and Texas, where the different command were and how many there were. While I was talking, who should enter the cabin but the Captain of the steamer *Lafuche*,[2] wishing to see the Gen'; as I was going out I had to pass the Captain. He looked at me as if he would like to eat me. The Gen' called his orderly to have me cleaned and new suit of clothes throughout.

First we went to a barber who was on board and had my hair cut, and face shaved. Next went to the wheel house to prepare for an entire clean change.[3] There was a number of the boys there, who came to see me, for I was a curious looking being, for my flesh had all turned black and blue where I had been laying on it and the boys busied themselves

2 Capt. William King skippered the *Lafourche* in early 1865. New Orleans *Daily True Delta*, Feb. 14, 1865: 1, retrieved from newspapers.com.

3 The wheelhouse was the structure enclosing the steering wheel of the ship. *Oxford English Dictionary.*

by picking up a little insect which is called a tick out of my back for my back was covered with them. The tick is a small bug that burries its head and shoulders under the skin, and cannot be pulled out by taking hold of their body, they will break off and leave their heads under the skin and makes a fester. They have to be picked out with a knife or they will fester and become very sore.

I got myself all cleaned and an entire new suit of clothing. I was weak and hungry. I went up into the cabin the officers had all left and I looked in the mirror which hung in the general's room and I was startled at my own self. I had not seen a glass for year and I had changed so that I should not have hardly known myself.[4]

I learned that the band on board was from Boston, and I went to look to see if there was any of them I knew. I found one young man who before the war was an intimate friend of mine. I spoke to him and he did not know me. I told him who I was. He did not recognize me. He asked if I was the fellow that came on board the boat about an hour ago, with rebel clothes on and long hair. I told him I was, and if he would come in the cabin a few moments I would convince him who I was. I told him of several incidents which happened while at home, and he soon began to look at me a little closer, and was soon convinced who I was.

I made friends with a great many, and they provided every thing for my comfort. The officers had been searching the steamer *Lafuche* and had taken the flags. I met several of the rebs after I had got my blue clothes on, and they looked hard at me. I lived well and enjoyed myself.

On the third day, the Gen' told me that the steamer *Lafuche*, was going to start for New Orleans, the next morning, and that he wanted me to go on her. He said that

---

4 In this sense, "glass" is a synonym for "mirror." *Oxford English Dictionary.*

Brig. Gen.
Thomas W. Sherman

Library of Congress

the same Captain and parolled men were going, and that would be the only chance for me for some time. He gave me two letters, one to the Provost Marshall[5] and another to Gen' Sherman, who was in command in New Orleans.[6]

The next morning I bade the Gen' and men good bye and went on board the steamer. I had a room to myself and three days rations all cooked. I was the only federal on board, and I feared they might have their revenge on me, now they had a chance. The Gen' assured me there was no fear of harming me, for there were boats all along the river and that I had a few friends on board.

5 The provost marshal was concerned with discipline and punishment of criminal activity among soldiers, and was in charge of conscription. Presumably, Federhen sought him out to avoid charges of desertion and to locate his unit. Wright, *The Language of the Civil War*, 239.

6 Brig. Gen. Thomas West "Tim" Sherman held command in the Southern District of Louisiana from Feb. 11 to Jun. 2, 1865. Eicher and Eicher, *Civil War High Commands*, 484.

36

REUNITED WITH
MY UNIT IN NEW ORLEANS
(JUNE 6, 1865)

ABOUT THE middle of the afternoon the boat started and I kept in my room not going on deck but once. We reached New Orleans in a few days it was evening, and after I landed, I went in search of the Provost Marshall. I found his quarters, but he had gone home.[1]

I wondered about the city sometime, and went into the camp of distribution for the night.[2] I found an empty bunk, lay on my blanket on the plank, and soon fell fast asleep. In the morning I fell in line with the other soldiers and got my rations. After I had eaten my breakfast, I looked for my letters but could not find them. I had lost them in the night out of my pocket. I took my blanket and started to go out of the yard

---

1 The provost marshal's office was on Carondelet Street at the corner of Perdido. William W. White, "Demobilization of Louisiana Confederate Forces, April–July 1865", in *The Civil War in Louisiana, Part A: Military Activity*, ed. Arthur W. Bergeron, Jr. (Lafayette: Center for Louisiana Studies, 2002), 568.

2 A camp of distribution served to house new recruits who had come down the Mississippi, before they were sent to their regiments. Leonard L. Lerwill, "The Personnel Replacement System in the United States Army" (Washington, DC: Department of the Army, 1954), 105.

(the camp was in a cotton press yard)[3] when I was stopped by the guard. I told him that I did not belong in there, and I wanted to go to the Provost Marshall's office. He said that I had no business in there then if I did not belong there, and he called the office of the guard. He came and said that it was against the rules, to let any one out without a pass. I told him that I arrived in the city late and I slept there last night. He wanted to know to what unit I belonged. I told him.[4] He said that the battery was stationed about six miles from the city, and that he would send a guard with me to it.[5] He brought out a man and we started off for the battery.

The guard had plenty of money, and he spent it freely for ice-creams, lemonade and etc. We did not reach the battery until afternoon, and but for a few of the men knew me. The first Lieut. was in command of the Battery, and the second day that I was in camp, I asked for a pass to go to the city.[6] It was refused and the Lieut. ordered me on the ground. I told him that I was not able to do duty, and that I wanted to go to the city to see a doctor. He said he would have me tied to the wheel if I gave him any talk, and so I went on duty.[7]

3 A cotton press was a machine that packed cotton into bales. *Oxford English Dictionary.*

4 Federhen had been assigned to the 13th Independent Battery, Massachusetts Light Artillery, before his capture. *Massachusetts Soldiers, Sailors, and Marines in the Civil War,* 1931.

5 The 13th Independent Battery was stationed at Greenville, which is now part of the Uptown neighborhood of New Orleans about five miles by foot upstream from the provost marshal's quarters. *OR* 48/1/1108.

6 In the spring of 1865, the officers were 1Lt. Charles B. Slack of Newton, Mass., and 2Lts. Chauncey R. Sias of Boston and James M. Lincoln of Taunton. Bowen, *Massachusetts in the War,* 851.

7 One punishment for artillerymen was to stretch out their arms and legs against the wheel of a caisson, and tie them against the rim; the soldier was left in that position for hours. Robert Bateman, "Crime and Punishment in

Col. Ormand F. Nims

Whitcomb, *History of the Second Massachusetts Battery (Nims' Battery) of Light Artillery: 1861–1865*

I stood duty all day, and next morning before roll call, I started without a pass to the city. I was arrested by the paroll guard and locked up for being in the city without a pass, to wait trial of court marshall as the clerks were going to their dinners, and I had to pass the sentry's door. I spoke to one of them, and asked him if he would go to a friend of mine who was in a governmental office and tell him I wanted to see him. He went and soon returned with my friend, Col. O. F. Nimms, one of the bravest and most successful officers in the service.[8]

the Civil War," *Esquire*, Nov. 14, 2013, www.esquire.com/news-politics/news/a25915/punishment-and-torture-in-the-civil-war-111413/.

8 Ormand F. Nims served with the 2nd Independent Battery, Massachusetts Light Artillery until Jan. 1865, when he resigned his commission. He remained in New Orleans for some time after he resigned, working with the quartermaster's department. Caroline E. Whitcomb, *History of the Second Massachusetts Battery (Nims' Battery) of Light Artillery: 1861–1865* (Concord, N.H.: Rumford Press, 1912), 76, 80; E. L. Patch, "Some Boston Druggists of Fifty Years Ago," *Journal of the American Pharmaceutical Association*, 10, no. 1 (Jan. 1921), 204.

He was much surprised, for he supposed I was dead. A very few words told him my situation and he went to the officers of the guard to get my release, but they could not without an order from General Sherman. He went immediately to Gen' Sherman, and after telling the General who I was and where I had been for over a year, the Gen' ordered my release and a pass to come to his quarters. I was soon released and stood before the Gen'. I sat down and told him what I had seen, and been through and told him about the letter from Gen' Herrin. He asked me the reason of my being in the city without a pass. I told him that I asked for one yesterday to come to the city to visit a doctor, to see about my ankle, and instead of a pass he ordered me on guard. I showed the Gen' my ankle for it was all raw and bleeding. He wanted to know how that happened. I told him that was where I had been ironed while a prisoner, under Gen' McCallough. The Gen' not having a very good opinion of my officers, for he had offered them off the field several times, for not being able to attend to duty.[9]

After talking some time he told his adjutant to write a pass exempting me from duty in camp, and a pass to come into the city every day until further orders. The Gen signed it, and handed it to me. I took it and left his guards. While I was going back to my camp the same paroll officer halted me again. I showed them my pass, and passed on. I went back to camp. The Lieut. wanted to know where I had been. I told him

9 The 13th Independent Battery was never directly under the command of T. W. Sherman during battle. Although it was attached to the 12th Massachusetts Battery during the Siege of Port Hudson in 1863, where Sherman was wounded, the 12th was under the command of Gen. Christopher Augur. After the end of the Red River Campaign, the unit was assigned to occupation duty for the duration of the war. Capt. Hamlin was dishonorably discharged after the war ended. Bowen, *Massachusetts in the War*, 851; David C. Edmonds, *The Guns of Port Hudson*, vol. 2: *The Investment, Siege, and Reduction* (Lafayette, LA: Acadiana Press, 1984), 387.

I had been to the city and had a pass signed by Gen' Sherman to be exempt from all duty of camp and to visit the city every day. He wanted to see the pass. I took it from my pocket, and handed it to him. After he had read it he crumpled it up and put it into his pocket. I asked him if he was not going to give it back to me again. He said that he would not, and if I did not go to my quarters, he would tie me up to the spare wheel. I left and went to my quarters.

In the morning after roll-call I started out of camp to go to the city. I had not got far out of camp before I heard someone after me. I turned and one of the boys came up, with a piece of paper in his hand. I opened it and it was my pass. The Lieut. was afraid I would report him so he sent it in time. After that the Lieut. had nothing more to say to me. I was always there at roll-call, and drew my rations.

37

RETURNING TO BOSTON
(JULY 14–21, 1865)

SOON THE order came to pack up and be ready to start for home. Just before we started, I wrote a few lines to my mother to let her know I was alive, for the report came home when I was captured, that I was last seen shot through the head, lying on the deck of the boat, together with all the dead and wounded, and the ship burned. When this news reached home they gave me up for dead, and I knew a few lines sent on before, would do more good than if I came in on them by surprise.

The battery and New York Company started one fine morning down the Mississippi River for home.[1] We were about eight days coming to New York. After we got into the gulf stream, there blew up a storm, and it was very rough, the rest of our passage. When we arrived in New York, they put us in the Battery camp that night.[2]

---

1 The *Hagar* departed New Orleans on Jul. 14 with the 13th Massachusetts Battery and the 25th New York Battery aboard, and docked in New York on Jul. 20. Philadelphia *Inquirer*, Jul. 21, 1865: 1, retrieved from ProQuest Historical Newspapers.

2 On the night of Jul. 20, the 13th Massachusetts Battery was quartered at the Battery Barracks, a complex constructed in 1863 to house 5,000 troops in the Battery section of Manhattan (now Battery Park). New York *Daily Tribune*, Jul. 21, 1865: 8, retrieved from ProQuest Historical

The next afternoon the Battery left New York for Boston. As soon as we landed in Boston, we were put under guard, while they were forming The Battery into line. I gave them the slip and ran for home. I found my mother in the kitchen, and when I opened the door she stood looking at me in wonder and astonishment, for I did not look as much as I did when I left home. I was pale and thin. I was heartily welcomed home, and soon I sat down to a good table with hot biscuit and Yankee coffee, prepared by a dear Mother who had surrendered both her sons to the altar of liberty, and had strove hard to do all she could for the soldiers comfort. My brother who was an officer in the first Mass. Battery, while engaged in a heavy battle was shot off his horse, and the news came that he was shot and taken off the battle field.[3] He was properly cared for and soon recovered. He had three bullets pass through his thighs, and his horse shot from under him.

The Battery had been sent to Galloups Island to wait for their discharge. We soon mustered out of the U.S. service, and were again citizens.[4]

Newspapers; Edward K. Spann, *Gotham at War: New York City, 1860–1865* (Wilmington, DE: SR Books, 2002), 67.

3 See "Biographical Note on W. F. Oscar Federhen and Family," on page xvi for a brief account of Jacob Federhen, Oscar's older brother.

4 The 13th Independent Battery was mustered out of service in Boston on Jul. 28, 1865. Gallops Island is one of the Boston Harbor islands. Bowen, *Massachusetts in the War*, 851.

POSTSCRIPT

VERY LITTLE is known about William Francis Oscar Federhen's postwar life.

At some point he became a member of the Gettysburg Post (Massachusetts Post No. 191) of the Grand Army of the Republic in Boston. On June 30, 1892, he filed an application for a pension as "invalid" and listed his service as "13 Indpt. Batty. Mass. L.A."[1]

He married Mary E. Wilder on January 1, 1867. According to existing records, he was 21 and she was 22 years old. His occupation was listed as clerk. They remained married until her death on April 27, 1906. On September 5, 1867, his son William Harrison Federhen was born in Boston. His daughter Lizzie was born in Boston on December 28, 1874.

From the end of the war through around 1904 Federhen lived in Boston or its suburbs of Somerville and Cohasset, though he spent time in Salina, Kansas, where his father-in-law had a home. He variously listed his profession as "clerk," "provisions dealer," or "sales." He was initiated into the Joseph Warren Masonic Lodge in Boston in 1872. In the early 1900s he moved to Salina, where he worked as a butcher or provisions dealer and rented out rooms. Between

---

1 Grand Army of the Republic Post Reports, 1880–1940; U.S., Civil War Pension Index: General Index to Pension Files, 1861–1934.

W. D. Oscar Federhen's grave.

Jeaninne Surette Honstein

1904 and 1919, Federhen was recorded as a member of the John A. Logan Post of the Grand Army of the Republic in Salina. By 1929, he had returned to Boston.

The aging veteran and former POW died of myocarditis, arteriosclerosis, and senility in Chelsea, Massachusetts, on October 2, 1933. His death certificate records his age as 88. He is interred beside his wife in Boston's Mount Hope Cemetery.[2]

2 1880 United States Federal Census; 1910 United States Federal Census; 1920 United States Federal Census; 1930 United States Federal Census; Mount Hope Cemetery records, Boston.

BIBLIOGRAPHY

PRIMARY SOURCES

BOOKS

Bartlett, John Russell. *Dictionary of Americanisms*. Boston: Little, Brown, and Co., 1877.

Brewer, E. Cobham. *Dictionary of Phrase and Fable*. New York: Cassell and Company, 1898.

Burke, Robert. *Escape from a Southern Prison*. No publisher or date recorded.

Cobb, Lyman. *The Reticule and Pocket Companion, Or, Miniature Lexicon of the English Language*. New York: Harper & Brothers, 1867.

Craighill, William P. *The Army Officer's Pocket Companion: Principally Designed for Staff Officers in the Field*. New York: D. Van Nostrand, 1862.

Dyer, Frederick H. *A Compendium of the War of the Rebellion* (Dayton, Morningside, 1978.

Forbes, John, Alexander Tweedie, and John Conolly, eds. *The Cyclopædia of Practical Medicine*. Philadelphia: Blanchard and Lea, 1859.

McElroy's Philadelphia City Directory for 1864. Philadelphia: E. C. & J. Biddle & Co., 1864.

Oxford Concise Medical Dictionary, 8th ed. New York: Oxford University Press, 2014.

Passmore, Augustine C. *Handbook of Technical Terms Used in Architecture and Building and their Allied Trades and Subject*. New York: D. Van Nostrand, 1904.

Swiggett, S. A. *The Bright Side of Prison Life*. Baltimore: Fleet, McGinley, & Co., 1897.

Taylor, Richard. *Destruction and Reconstruction: Personal Experiences of the Late War*. New York: D. Appleton and Co., 1879.

GOVERNMENT DOCUMENTS

Lerwill, Leonard L. "The Personnel Replacement System in the United States Army." Washington, DC: Department of the Army, 1954.

Massachusetts Adjutant General's Office. *Massachusetts Soldiers, Sailors, and Marines in the Civil War*. Norwood, MA: Norwood Press, 1931.

Official Army Register of the Volunteer Force of the United States Army for the Years 1861, '62, '63, '64, '65, Part IV: *Texas*. Washington, DC, Government Printing Office, 1865.

Official Records of the Union and Confederate Navies in the War of the Rebellion. Washington, DC: Government Printing Office, 1894–1922.

United States House of Representatives. Report No. 45, *Report on the Treatment of Prisoners of War, by the Rebel Authorities, during the War of the Rebellion*. Washington, DC: Government Printing Office, 1869.

NEWSPAPERS

Saline County Journal (Salina, Kansas).

Newspapers.com Library Edition.

ProQuest Historical Newspapers, library database.

DATABASES

Ancestry.com Library Edition.

Fire Insurance Maps Online, library database.

National Park Service. "Soldiers and Sailors Database." www.nps.gov /civilwar /soldiers-and-sailors-database.htm.

Oxford English Dictionary, library database.

SECONDARY SOURCES

BOOKS

Allardice, Bruce S. Confederate Colonels: A Biographical Register. Columbia: University of Missouri Press, 2008.

Bowen, James L. Massachusetts in the War, 1861-1865. Springfield, MA: C. W. Bryan & Co., 1889.

Bryan, Jimmy L. More Zeal Than Discretion: The Westward Adventures of Walter P. Lane. College Station: Texas A&M University Press, 2008.

Castel, Albert, and Thomas Goodrich. Bloody Bill Anderson: The Short, Savage Life of a Civil War Guerilla. Mechanicsburg, PA: Stackpole, 1998.

Collins, Ace. Songs Sung Red, White, and Blue: The Stories Behind America's Best-Loved Patriotic Songs. New York: HarperResource, 2003.

Collins, Robert. General James G. Blunt: Tarnished Glory. Gretna, LA: Pelican Publishing Co., 2005.

Cunningham, Edward. The Port Hudson Campaign, 1862-1863. Baton Rouge: Louisiana State University Press, 1963.

Cutrer, Thomas W. Theater of a Separate War: The Civil War West of the Mississippi River, 1861-1865. Chapel Hill: University of North Carolina Press, 2017.

Edmonds, David C. The Guns of Port Hudson, vol. 2, The Investment, Siege, and Reduction. Lafayette, LA: Acadiana Press, 1984.

Eicher, John E., and David J. Eicher. Civil War High Commands. Stanford, CA: Stanford University Press, 2001.

Gibson, Charles Dana, and E. Kay Gibson. Dictionary of Transports and Combatant Vessels, Steam and Sail, Employed by the Union Army, 1861-1868. Camden, ME: Ensign Press, 1995.

Gittinger, Roy. The Formation of the State of Oklahoma. Norman: University of Oklahoma Press, 1939.

Goodman, Jordan, ed. Tobacco in History and Culture. Detroit: Thomson Gale, 2005.

Hämäläinen, Pekka. The Comanche Empire. New Haven: Yale University Press, 2008.

Haskin, William L. The History of the First Regiment of Artillery from Its Organization in 1821, to January 1, 1876. Portland, ME: B. Hurston & Co., 1879.

Johnson, Robert Underwood, and Clarence Clough Buel, eds. Battles and Leaders of the Civil War, vol. I. New York: The Century Co., 1884.

Joiner, Gary D. Through the Howling Wilderness: The 1864 Red River Campaign and Union Failure In the West. Knoxville: University of Tennessee Press, 2006.

Lawrence, F. Lee, and Robert W. Glover. Camp Ford, C.S.A.: The Story of Union Prisoners in Texas. Austin: Texas Civil War Centennial Advisory Committee, 1964.

Leslie, Edward E. The Devil Knows How to Ride: The True Story of William Clarke Quantrill and His Confederate Raiders. New York: Random House, 1996.

Lord, Francis A. Uniforms of the Civil War. South Brunswick, NJ: Thomas Yoseloff, 1970.

Maxwell, William Quentin. Lincoln's Fifth Wheel: The Political History of the United States Sanitary Commission. New York: Longmans, Green, 1956.

McCaslin, Richard B. Tainted Breeze: The Great Hanging at Gainesville, Texas, 1862. Baton Rouge: Louisiana State University Press, 1994.

Morgan, James F. Graybacks and Gold: Confederate Monetary Policy. Pensacola, FL: Perdido Bay Press, 1985.

Noirsain, Serge. Les guerres indiennes du Texas et du Nouveau-Mexique: 1825-1875. Paris: Economica, 2011.

Phisterer, Frederick. Statistical Record of the Armies of the United States. Campaigns of the Civil War. New York: Charles Scribner's Sons, 1883.

Prushankin, Jeffrey S. *A Crisis in Confederate Command: Edmund Kirby Smith, Richard Taylor, and the Army of the Trans-Mississippi.* Baton Rouge: Louisiana State University Press, 2005.

Roberts, George. *The Terms and Language of Trade and Commerce, and of the Business of Every-Day Life.* London: Longman, Orme, Brown, Green, and Longmans, 1841.

Sargent, Dean. *Grand Army of the Republic: Civil War Veterans, Department of Massachusetts, 1866 to 1947.* Bowie, MD: Heritage Books, 2002.

Schroeder-Lein, Glenna R. *The Encyclopedia of Civil War Medicine.* Armonk, NY: M.E. Sharpe, 2008.

Schultz, Duane. *Quantrill's War: The Life and Times of William Clarke Quantrill, 1837-1865.* New York: St. Martin's Press, 1996.

Shurtleff, Nathaniel B. *A Topographical and Historical Description of Boston,* 2nd ed. Boston: Noyes, Holmes, and Co., 1872.

Smith, David Paul. *Frontier Defense in the Civil War: Texas' Rangers and Rebels.* College Station: Texas A&M University Press, 1992.

Soman, Jean Powers, and Frank L. Byrne, eds. *A Jewish Colonel in the Civil War: Marcus M. Spiegel of the Ohio Volunteers.* Lincoln: University of Nebraska Press, 1995.

Spann, Edward K. *Gotham at War: New York City, 1860-1865.* Wilmington, DE: SR Books, 2002.

Sullivan, David M. *The United States Marine Corps in the Civil War,* vol. 1: *The First Year.* Shippensburg, PA: White Mane Publishing Co., 1997.

Sutton, Aaron T. *Prisoner of the Rebels in Texas: The Civil War Narrative of Aaron T. Sutton.* Edited by David G. MacLean. Decatur, IN: Americana Books, 1978.

Whayne, Jeannie M., Thomas A. DeBlack, George Sabo, and Morris S Arnold. *Arkansas: A Narrative History,* 2nd ed. Fayetteville: University of Arkansas Press, 2013.

Whitcomb, Caroline E. *History of the Second Massachusetts Battery (Nims' Battery) of Light Artillery: 1861-1865.* Concord, NH: Rumford Press, 1912.

White, William W. "Demobilization of Louisiana Confederate Forces, April–July 1865." In *The Civil War in Louisiana,* Part A: *Military Activity,* edited by Arthur W. Bergeron, Jr., 564-71. Lafayette: Center for Louisiana Studies, 2002.

Wooster, Ralph A. *Lone Star Regiments in Gray.* Austin, TX: Eakin Press, 2002.

Wright, John D. *The Language of the Civil War.* Westport, CT: Greenwood, 2001.

ARTICLES

Bateman, Robert. "Crime and Punishment in the Civil War." *Esquire,* November 14, 2013. http://www.esquire.com/news-politics/news/a25915/punishment-and-torture-in-the-civil-war-111413/

"The Crow." *Connecticut School Journal* 7, no. 26 (1902): 7–8.

"Major General F. J. Herron." *Annals of Iowa* 5, no. 1 (January 1867): 801–807.

Patch, E. L. "Some Boston Druggists of Fifty Years Ago." *Journal of the American Pharmaceutical Association,* 10, no. 1 (January 1921): 204.

Scarborough, W. S. "Negro Dialect in Fiction." *Unitarian Review,* 32, no. 1 (July 1889): 77–83.

Smyrl, Frank H. "Texans in the Union Army, 1861-1865." *Southwestern Historical Quarterly,* 65 (1961): 234–50.

DISSERTATIONS AND THESES

Snyder, Perry Anderson. "Shreveport, Louisiana, during the Civil War and Reconstruction." Ph.D. dissertation, Florida State University, 1979.

INDEX

This index uses currently accepted spellings for personal names and places, even where Federhen's text uses an alternate spelling.

Acknowledgments

Technical notes: We are grateful to the staff of the Massachusetts Historical Society for sharing copies of *The Old Flag* with us and to Wangyal Shawa for his assistance in creating our map. The estate of Lee Lawrence kindly granted us permission to reprint the map from *Camp Ford, C.S.A.*

The folks at Savas Beatie, including its director, Theodore P. Savas, marketing director Sarah Keeney, publicist Sarah Closson, account managers Donna Endacott and Lisa Murphy, copy editor Joel Manuel, and production manager Lee Merideth, have all done outstanding work transforming this manuscript into a very handsome book and pushing it out into the market.

Personal notes from Jeaninne Surette Honstein: I am grateful for my mother's devotion to genealogical research and for my parent's love of history. Without them, I don't know if I would have ever started this project.

I am grateful to those who helped me at the New England Historic Genealogical Society and the Massachusetts Historical Society.

Without Ancestry.com, it would have taken me years to find information for this project.

To Anne Jarvis, a wonderful neighbor and friend who happens to be the Princeton University Librarian who introduced me to Steven A. Knowlton. How lucky is that?

To my dear friend Ann Behar for donating her time and helping to steer us in a positive direction when it came time to work with our publisher, Savas Beatie, who I would like to thank for agreeing to publish this memoir.

To my friends, family, children, and spouses who listened to me and shared my excitement.

To Steven Knowlton, who could not be a better partner to work with. He was very kind and generous with his time. He is succinct and enthusiastic about the project. He worked hard to annotate and find our publisher. Once he had the manuscript in hand, he knew exactly what to do with it. Through his connections, resources, and determination, I am grateful that this manuscript is now being published and made available to the reading public.

And to my husband Robert, for his support, encouragement, and all the times I said I could not go out because I was "working on something." Thank you for your patience and love.

About the Editors

JEANINNE HONSTEIN is a conceptual artist based in Princeton, New Jersey. Her paintings, sculpture, photography, and writing are influenced by her perception of history and antiquities. She is pleased to bring the story of her ancestor William Francis Oscar Federhen to the attention of the reading public for the first time.

STEVEN A. KNOWLTON is Librarian for History and African American Studies at Princeton University. His historical research has been published in many peer-reviewed journals. He is the recipient of the William Driver Award from the North American Vexillological Association and the Marshall Wingfield Award from the West Tennessee Historical Society, and has won the Justin Winsor Library History Essay Award twice. This is his first book.